ODDLY BODLIKINS

PAUL JENNINGS

ODDLY BODLIKINS

Illustrations by Haro Hodson

MAX REINHARDT

LONDON

First Published 1953

Printed at
THE STELLAR PRESS LTD.
BARNET, HERTS

*To the doctors and nurses in Coventry and London who
saved our baby, Susanna*

My thanks are due for permission to reprint to the Editors of *Time and Tide* (The Persian Rug Crisis) *House and Garden* (Advice to Husbands) *Family Doctor* (Harley Street) *The Advertiser's Weekly* (Clangpan's Copy).

They are also due to the Editor of *The Observer* not only for permission to reprint the *Oddly Enough's* which make up the rest of the volume, but also for creating a climate in which it is possible to write them.

P.F.J.

CONTENTS

(*Continued overleaf*)

THE FANG MANAGERS

There is always something mildly exciting about a Census. As this vast numbering-off-from-the-right of a whole nation proceeds, there are placid jokes in many homes as the elderly man on the bicycle asks who is the head of the household. There is a geniality about our ten-yearly encounters with these temporary employees of the General Register Office that reminds us of the cheerful, unprofessional auxiliary postmen at Christmas. And even the permanent staff, at Southport and Somerset House, seem the most innocuous of all Civil Servants, as they sit there among their dusty files, quietly adding us all up.

For it *is* a quaint picture that they have of us. I have just been reading the stupendous catalogue which they were using as a basis for coding clerks in the Census – the *Classification of Occupations*, 1950. It is a large blue book, foolscap size, nearly an inch thick. It costs 13s. 6d. It makes a valiant attempt to list every trade and occupation in these islands – *and* to grade them in social classes. And it is the most fascinating Government publication I have ever read, which is saying something.

The people who compiled this vast work seem to have gone about workshops and factories and mines collecting the names of dying and esoteric crafts with the apostolic zeal of a Cecil Sharp collecting folk songs. There are gems on every page. Glad Ironer, Big Back Bender, Botcher, Fat Boy, Plonking Machinist, Sad Iron Grinder; Slubber, Slugger, Slosher, Snob; Balloon Minder, Puff Putter-in, Bonker, Boomer; Sweating House Foreman, Face Grinder, Odd Stamper, Alpine Lad; Blood Collector, Carrier-Away, Fang Manager, Hont Loader; Hanger-on, Tricycle Maker, Bacon Expert, Poet, Layer-out of the Dead; Legger in Tunnel, Hobbler to Dock Pilots; Gimp Lapper, Belly Roller, Blow Major, Bumble Man . . .

It is tantalising, as well as fascinating, to read this book. On the very first page we have Trolloper, Whammeller, Husbandman (in Wales), Marsh Looker, Woman Gardener, Lady Gardener and Exotic Gardener. Immediately the mind is full of unanswered questions. Is there some unknown feudal enclave in Wales, with Husbandmen in smocks? Or is it that *English* Husbandmen, with their motor cycles and television sets, refused point-blank to be thus bucolically described? And what of the Woman Gardener, a buxom figure like a Russian policewoman; the Lady Gardener, snipping daintily in her housecoat; and the Exotic Gardener, among his tinkling fountains and heavy, swooning oriental blooms? How does the Census man deal with an obvious Woman Gardener's claim that she is a Lady Gardener? And what is a Whammeller?

But we must leave them regretfully, for our endless tour of small, dark, nineteenth-century factories and old mines. For there is an extraordinarily old-fashioned air about the book, as the compilers themselves are uneasily aware; they say in their Introduction that ' it has been necessary to be conservative over the omission of apparently obsolete terms, since many old people now retired may still make use of these terms.' Here they give themselves away. If these old people *are* retired, surely there's no need to include their occupations, such as Hearing Trumpet Maker, Black Scraping Man, Tommy Dodd Mangler, Mrs. Shifter, Dewdropper.

Obviously these old people should be among the Retired from Gainful Occupation (part of a splendid page where the book ends with a dazzling finale of Other and No Occupations – Bellman, Articulator of Bones and Skeletons, Jack of All Trades, Maggot Breeder, Capitalist, Gentleman, Usher, Gipsy, Graduate; Lunatic, Trade Not Stated.) Evidently these Civil Servants, raising their polite voices among the clamour of antique machinery, slightly self-conscious of their city clothes and white collars, were simply seduced by the ancient music of these names.

I suspect, also, that sometimes they have fallen for old workshop jokes. I am sure that in different trades, clumsy or useless workmen are referred to varyingly as Crocus Polisher, Plug and Feather Man, Starlight Maker (obviously a dreamy fellow who keeps dropping nuts and bolts), Beaming Lad, or Quilt Banger (analogous to the old Indian Army's charpoy basher, a man who is always asleep on his charpoy or bed).

Some of the jobs sound so simple that it is difficult to believe they are well paid enough to be worth anybody's while. Such are Runner-Away, Puller-to-Pieces (Book),

Sickle Wrapper, Card Wire Giver-Out, Rider on Top and Scissors Wiper. I am sure these working parties that go to America to study efficiency have never found any Scissors Wipers *there*.

I see I have left hardly any room for the Horror Dept.—Bogey Man, Dreep Man (obviously an awful damp Thing lurking in cellars), Burnt Out Man, Decomposing Man, Boogie Man, Wet Rubber Man, Blood Pudding Maker, Head Splitting Operator . . .

But then *I* haven't got 317 pages.

IRON WALKING STICKS

There is something curiously indeterminate about the sound of Afghanistan. The very name, with the clear, basic beginning *afghan* blown away by the rushing *istan*, suggests one of those little whirling pools of dry dust – dust like that suspended in the sharp, bright air of a winter afternoon in the northern Punjab, where huge mountains, with ice and forests, feed India's holy rivers before giving way in the west to an ennui of rocky hills.

We know that Tibet, precise, definite and hieratic, is behind the Himalayas, but we can never remember the shape of Afghanistan, if it has one. We can remember none of its towns. We expect it to be blindingly hot, but we feel that if we went there we should see people wearing coloured blankets on a cloudy day. Through the dust of

hooves we see bazaars, and tribesmen, and carpets. An
uneasy, formless country, halfway to Russia; a country full
of magnificent *individuals*, with black, drooping moustaches.

Let us now, against this background, consider an
announcement made not long ago in the *Board of Trade
Journal* that ' the British Embassy in Kabul ' (yes, that's
it, Kabul, of course) ' has reported that the Afghan
authorities have prohibited the import of some hundred
articles in an effort to maintain equilibrium between their
imports and exports.' This hundred includes:

> Jams (all kinds)
> Reed tubes for hubble bubbles
> Walking sticks (iron)
> Celluloid ear-rings
> Various kinds of stars
> Looking glasses (certain large sizes)
> Woad leaves (hair dyes)
> Purgative manna
> Metal utensils made in Muradabad
> Vermicelli machines

—and underneath it says that previously the only prohibited articles were ' certain types of books . . . all kinds
of poisons, opium, morphine, cocaine, hashish, wine and
all other intoxicants (*with exceptions to cater for foreigners in
the country*).' My italics.

At first sight this extraordinary list would seem to be a
protest at the outside world's easy assumption that it can
sell any old thing in Afghanistan. We may imagine some
Afghan civil servant, with degrees from Manchester and
the Massachusetts Institute of Technology, ringing up our
Embassy and saying ' Look here, old boy, I do wish you'd
tell your people that what we want in this country is turbo-
alternators, and plenty of 'em. Another shipment of

celluloid ear-rings and purgative manna turned up yesterday; and No. 2 Bonded Warehouse is crammed full with
those wretched vermicelli machines.'

But when we look more closely the dust cloud rises
again; through it we get fragmentary, tantalising glimpses
of these foreigners, crazy, dissolute, selling the tribesmen
arms thinly disguised as iron walking sticks (it is character-
istically confusing that this expression suggests the South
Seas rather than Afghanistan. *Big feller iron walking stick,
him go bang along topside.*) Perhaps the vermicelli machines
are for the Italian cafés where these foreigners pass each
other notes and hashish under the table.

Another obvious difficulty is why hard-headed British
business men should ever have considered crazy enterprises
like selling reed tubes for hubble bubbles to Afghanistan.
It sounds exactly like selling coals to Newcastle. Can it be
that these foreigners are once able commercial agents
whose business acumen is now dulled by opium?

One sees the Sales Manager back at home, taking a
cable in to the Managing Director. It reads: PIPECRAFT
WOLVERHAMPTON RUSH FOUR MILLION HUBLE
BUBLE WAT SILY WORD HUBLE BUBLE REED TUBES
EARLIEST REGARDS PHILLIPS HUBLE BUBLE AHA
HA HA PHILLIPS. 'A bit odd, J.B.' he says ' still, Phillips
is one of our best men – look at that order for a suspension
bridge he got us in Tristan da Cunha. I'd back his judg-
ment anywhere.' And all the time Phillips, his hair blue
with woad, is chattering with delirium in a dusty tent,
seeing various kinds of stars.

And what is this feud with Muradabad? Has bitter
experience proved that these worthless metal utensils are
full of holes? Or that, melted down, they make feeble iron
walking sticks which explode with the first bullet? Or has

Afghanistan followed the example of larger nations, conducting, instead of a wild raid on Muradabad, a cold economic war? It seems less picturesque than the flying hooves, the dust, the rifle cracks in the stony valley . . .

IT'S SLOWER BY BALLOON

In view of the present crisis in transport, the Report of the Royal Commission set up to examine the proposals for a State balloon line makes a timely appearance. In spite of the dry, official language of the Report, it is easy to imagine the effect on our landscape and travelling habits if it is adopted. There will be the calm, lofty buildings of the new balloon terminals, with anchors, and red and green spheres on white spars, like sharp paintings by Edward Wadsworth. A windy, Aeolian thrumming will be heard above the subdued voices of passengers asking for ' two to Montgomeryshire, please ' – since the most accurate wind forecast will permit no preciser destination.

We may imagine the dreamy passengers, in their wicker baskets, so reminiscent of picnic hampers, consuming ham,

B

port and cheese as their shadow flits over villages and towns; a silent, drifting traffic over the broad fields of England, like vague, half-formed thoughts sailing through a mind on the point of sleep. Balloony loony moony . . .

But the Report is less concerned with the atmosphere of ballooning than with a sober appraisal of its economics. The advantages are obvious. There is complete silence, in an increasingly noisy age. There is no expensive maintenance. The fuel is hydrogen, which, as every schoolboy knows, is easily made by passing steam over red-hot coke.

Both these commodities are plentiful at gasworks, and the Report says 'theoretically any town with a gasworks may have a balloon terminal. As, however, gasworks are usually found in crowded, unattractive districts, it is recommended that the hydrogen be brought by pipeline to some pleasant spot on the outskirts, such as a park or a disused cemetery.'

The word ' theoretically ' is important, for it leads us to the crucial disadvantage of ballooning as a *scheduled* service – the instability of our prevailing winds. However, ' Air Ministry records show that the south-west wind reaches a 35 per cent. maximum in August, whereas east winds are more common in winter.' This may be turned to advantage in helping us to decide the class of public who are potential balloon travellers; a fairly well-to-do minority with strong individual tastes.

Winter is the season when most people come up to London. In August there is heavy rail and road traffic from the Midlands to Devonshire and the southwest – *i.e.* in the *opposite* direction to the prevailing winds. Advertising should therefore be directed at those who want to be different from the crowd, to go the other way. Summer regional advertising in the south-west should employ such

slogans as TIRED OF TRIPPERS? BORED WITH BANDS?
BRITISH BALLOONWAYS TAKES YOU AWAY FROM IT
ALL, AND DOESN'T BRING YOU BACK.'

The objection that such passengers might find themselves cooped up in baskets with the very Midlanders they
seek to avoid, returning home, ladies from trim white
houses in Torquay being matily offered pork pie by brass-
founders from Stechford, is foreseen by the recommenda-
tion that there be no transferability of return rail tickets.

Behind the dreamy atmosphere of ballooning there will
be a great deal of modern, high-pressure commercial
planning, with the accent on flexibility. When unexpected
southerly gales arise, loud speaker vans will tour the streets
advertising ' Suprise Trips to Scotland or thereabouts.'
Deflation plant will be installed in ' reception areas,' which
the wind is always blowing to and never from. From here
balloons, neatly folded, will be sent by road back to ' des-
patch areas.'

Just as the economic payload of aircraft is worked out by
skilled accountants, so will the profit from ' concentration
areas ' with a Montgolfier Factor of + 1 (i.e. areas such as
Wales, proved by an independent survey outside a football
ground in a typical London borough, Twickenham, one
Saturday afternoon, to be a place where more people
would like to go than wouldn't) be set against the compen-
sation to be paid to those who land unexpectedly at Fon-
tainebleau or Bad Hildesheim.

This comprehensive Report contains many technical
details. It recommends a modification of the war-time
balloon, fitted with saloon baskets and radiograms to play
Mozart. Alternatively, the Commission has examined the
proposal that the cables of each balloon should be tuned to
utter a characteristic note, component of an overall har-

monic scheme, so that the upper air would always rever-
berate with a far-off twangling, analogous to the ancient
music of the spheres. It also points out that Britain, with its
large stock of war-time balloons and of winds, is in a
unique position to lead the world in this enterprise.

Neither France nor Germany are yet in a position to
revive their pre-war organisations, the *Ballon d'Alsace* and
the *Luftgazbagverein*. We should not let this opportunity
slip.

QUO VADIS

In the first half-hour after I have left a theatre I am always convinced that I am going to write a play. It is a curious sensation, because I never know what the play is to be about. I just have a general impression, and yet at the same time a very clear one, of dramatic confrontations, of sharp, agonised words cutting into the hearts of a tense audience, without ever knowing what the words actually are.

This doesn't happen at the cinema. There is too much machinery in the way. However moving the film, one will also have seen a newsreel (when I go it always seems to contain a waiters' race in Paris) and a trailer, with little cameos of people being slapped, or surprised in embraces.

One remembers all the time that the film is just one more activity of this teeming world.

Yet this week, utterly illogically, I was inspired to write a film, too. I wasn't actually inspired by the film, but by the stills and posters on the mufflled way out; for these were to advertise M.G.M.'s ' Quo Vadis.' They all looked curiously unreal. I thought of the queue in togas at the studio restaurant, of the obvious gap between modern America and ancient Rome. And it was then that I thought of my film, which will bridge this gap by having the dialogue in Latin.

It is called *Balbi Murus*, ' The Wall of Balbus.' It is the story of a young engineer, Balbus, who has been commissioned by a Government agency, known by its initials SPQR, to build a wall, that the city may be defended against the Carthaginians. It is the story of his love for Julia (*Balbus amat Juliam*) who is the daughter of Marcellus, a prominent member of the SPQR. It also tells of the lone fight of these three against big-time graft in the heart of the world's mightiest empire. But read on.

The film opens with Marcellus making a passionate speech to the wavering SPQR, who have already delayed their decision about the wall for three years. He warns of the danger from the Carthaginians, and ends with a great peroration. This is above politics, he says. *Hoc est aliquid magnum, majus omnibus nobis. Per totam orbem, sunt milia milia populorum; parvi populi, solum similes nobis, cum hoc spe in cordibus suis.* (' This is something big, bigger than all of us. All over the world there are millions of people; little people just like you and me, with this hope in their hearts . . . ')

The SPQR applaud warmly. The contract is given to Balbus, and it is while they are crowding round to congratulate him that he first sees Julia. It is love at first sight.

Nonne[1] *aliquis tibi dixit te pulchram esse?* (' Did anyone ever tell you you're beautiful? ') he asks. He dates her for the evening. *Ego te feram ad parvum locum quem cognosco, solum nos duo.* (I'll take you to a little place I know, just the two of us '). *Ubi fuistis omnem vitam meam?* asks Julia. (Where have you been all my life? ').

But this idyll is shattered by the machinations of a grafter called Cæsar Romerus, of whom he has already been warned by Julia, *Iste homo est periculosus* (' That man is dangerous '). Romerus puts the word about that Marcellus, who is a stone merchant, is supplying Balbus with faked stones, made of plaster, for the wall. Balbus, angered by the rumours, goes down to inspect the wall, and finds to his horror that they *are* faked stones.

That night, dining with Julia, he is moody. *Num*[2] *est altera mulier?* (' Is there another woman? ') she asks. He confesses his doubts about her father's honesty, and there is a quarrel in which he accuses her of making love to him to shield Marcellus. *Nolo talem amorem* (' I don't want that kind of love ') *O mel, da mihi fracturam, et tibi demonstrabo quod non est vere* (' Gee, honey, give me a break, and I'll prove it isn't true '). *Mel, debes audire,* she implores (' Honey, you've got to listen ').

But Balbus is unmoved. He rises stiffly. *Hoc est vale,* (' This is goodbye ') he grates. Broken-hearted, Julia walks home alone. She hears voices coming from a cellar, and listens. It is Romerus and his associates, who are in league with the Carthaginians, plotting to substitute more fake stones. Startled, she cries, *Sic illud est ludus tuus* (' So that's your game ').

Romerus hears the intruder, and she is caught. *Tu mane ex hoc, soror* (' You stay out of this sister '), he snarls as she is kidnapped. Next day, in a Rome worried by the

---

[1] Question expecting the answer Yes.
[2] Question expecting the answer No.

news that the enemy is throwing forces across the river, a repentant Balbus is frantic at Julia's disappearance . . .

It would spoil the suspense of this mighty drama to reveal how Balbus, on bail awaiting a corruption charge with Marcellus, tracks down Romerus and rescues Julia. *Cape illud* (' Take that ') he grits, as his fist rams home on the grafter's chin; and how the pair, dishevelled but reunited, arrive at a dramatic moment in the trial of Marcellus. But look out for the posters:

Nunc, BALBI MURUS, maximum spectaculum omnis temporis. (Now, THE WALL OF BALBUS, the greatest spectacle of all time . . .)

TUNED CIRCUIT

Now that sacrilege against the BBC is being seriously contemplated, it is time to consider the whole business of broadcasting on a profounder plane than the purely social or economic. Intuitively, man has always known about radio – far more intuitively than he has known about the steam engine, for instance, which was already a clear intellectual concept to Archimedes. Radio is different.

The Greeks had other means than ours of tuning-in to the silent harmonies of the air. Look at their legend of Psyche, transported to the lonely palace of Eros in the Vale of Tempe – a palace in which celestial music came from nowhere. We have always known about radio. Just as the individual man, according to Plato, never learns anything new but rediscovers it, *remembers* it, so the human

race as a whole has had this remembering, this ' anamnesis,' of radio.

Today, the air about us is filled with foreign opera
companies, with Frenchmen gabbling news and beating a
little tingy gong (or perhaps a gongy ting), with audiences
laughing inexplicably at Dutch comedians, with unidentified, whispering Mozart; and the means by which
any one of these is isolated and realised is, fundamentally,
British. It is in fact, the tuned circuit, which allows one
wavelength only to pass, given by the formula $1885 \sqrt{LC}$,
where L is the inductance of a coil in microhenrys and C is
the capacity of a condenser in microfarads.

In every wireless set in the world Faraday and Henry
are there; *das Heinrich, le henri, el farado* (with the possible
exception of Russia, where L C doubtless stands for Lenin
and Ctalin). Henry it is true, was an American, but he was
born of Scottish parents. And let us give due honour to
Marconi, in stiff black clothes, receiving the dramatic
signals on that cliff in Cornwall, or wherever it was. But
Faraday, who practically invented electricity, comes first.
In the terms of this vast human anamnesis of radio, the
order of importance is Faraday, then this Henry, then
Marconi.

Radio, then, is something more than a box of tricks. At
its present stage of development it is halfway between
Psyche's magic music and pure cold science, mere television. It still has strong intuitive connections with folk
consciousness. In any foreign revolution, the rebels always
announce with mingled pride and guilt that they have
captured the radio station, which is like violating a sanctuary. And the BBC, full of empty corridors, lofty, dignified,
priestlike, its transmitter masts humming celestially in the
night wind over high land in the Midlands and West, has

this ' national ' claim to inviolacy as well as its historical claim, with these farads and machenrys, to be world radio what Wimbledon still is to world tennis.

Our radio sets are half reality and half fantasy. Mine has a little glass window on which are painted, in green, such absurd names as LILLE, BEROMUNSTER, ABERDEEN, STUTTGART. Are we really to believe that these are actual stations? Has anybody ever heard a voice say *Ici Lille*, or even ' Here is Aberdeen? ' And why is it that, unless we make the conscious effort of consulting the ' Radio Times,' whenever we turn on the BBC it is always *talking?* Music, in this fantasy folk world, is allocated to some opera house in Yugoslavia, always performing little known but intensely dramatic works, or to our friends the Dutch, always just finishing a choral work, or to Toulouse, always prattling away with a three-piece accordion band in 3/4 time.

The BBC, with the Third, Home and Light, the voice of the real us, with our multifarious tastes, stands firm on the middle wave-band, between the short wave, with those unsatisfactory coming-and-going stations, and the long wave, practically a desert except for a girl reading something about ten-tenths cloud in a monotonous voice. But consider how even the BBC, whose ' Radio Times ' is printed in familiar Wembley, is hedged about, even on the Home Service (on my set anyway), with lost spirits that start on a low grunt, rising, without my touching the set, to a wavering note around 800 cycles.

Consider the world of atmospherics – the little lost choirs singing oratorios, such as the *Me-eh-eh-si-i-ah-ah*, at the bottom of wells, the frantic guttural whisperings, the lunatic distorted pianos, the tinny orchestras of little men four inches high, grigging and twinking away on nutshell instruments, in a pink and green light down on the edge of

the world. The BBC, national, communing with Faraday
and Henry, knows about these things, and we interfere at
our peril.

BRABABOATS

I can't help feeling that there is omething unreal about the Brabazon and those even more mysterious creatures, the Princess Flying Boats. It is true that the Brabazon has flown, bumbling over London out of the silvery mist of Atlantis, out of the western Celtic dream where it lives with other fabulous British monsters. It is true that devoted craftsmen have worked on it, and that much useful theoretical knowledge has been gathered. But it is hardly possible to associate the ordinary aircraft industry, turning out brisk, efficient, and reasonably sized things like the Comet, and, soon, the even better Bristol 175, with this vast, confusing, dreamlike project which never seems to reach completion.

For one thing, there are so many people besides the makers concerned; and one gets the impression that they all behave like preoccupied Chekhov characters. 'Ah, when will the Brabazon be ready?' they ask, while, outside, the airframe riveters rattle with a sad sound, like the axes in the Cherry Orchard. It is as though the very names had hypnotized them. *Brabazon, Brabazon,* they say, in deep mournful voices, a whole vague crowd of them, like a stage crowd saying *rhubarb, rhubarb. Brabazon, Brabazon,* like the heavy murmuring of bees on a drugged, Tristan-and-Isolde summer afternoon.

And if Princess Flying Boats sound like anything real at all, it is the highly painted swings at a fair, like immediate candidates for the Aeronautical Museum at Kensington, among other endearing fantasies such as that French aerial canoe.

Lured by their fatal vision, the experts swarm all over the vast, bulbous machine as it grows; they are like the people in Breughel's painting of the Tower of Babel, all in the furious yet shadowy activity of a dream. *Brabazon, boats, Flying Brabazon, Brabazz, bzz, bzz, braba, braba, bzz . . .*

No, no, this is ridiculous. This is the twentieth century. There must be some simple explanation. Let us examine the facts. The Civil Appropriation Accounts, 1950-51. That seems prosaic enough:

'*Three Princess Flying Boats were ordered by the Ministry of Civil Aviation in* 1946 *at an estimated cost of* £2,800,000. *By June,* 1950, *the estimated cost had gone up to* £10,800,00 –' Well, cigarettes went up too. We follow so far. But to continue, '– *the machines had originally been intended for BOAC, but in October,* 1949, *BOAC undertook to purchase only the three airframes under construction for* £700,000 *each.*' Just a minute now. 3 × £700,000 is £2,100,000, which leaves £8,700,000 of that £10,800,000 for the engines. H'm. Ah, but this was in 1949. Oh well. '*After a further review in* 1951 *it was*

*decided that BOAC would not take them but that they should be
completed for the Royal Air Force, the Air Ministry paying not
more than £2,000,000. In December, 1951, the Air Ministry
withdrew its earlier request to the Ministry of Supply . . . '*

It's no good, we get lost half-way through this paragraph; it sounds like ' What has gone before ' in some
incredibly complicated serial. What is this Ministry of
Supply, turning up at the end like the uncle from Austra-
lia?

*" Meanwhile the Ministry of Insurance, warned by Sir Jasper
of BOAC's past, agrees to persuade the Metropolitan Water
Board to subsidise three new engines at a cost of £7 million. Then,
late one night, the Minister of Transport, driving to his country
home, sees an ominous red glow from the hangars. Now read
on . . . '*

It is impossible, reading this account, not to feel that
these monstrous aeroplanes infect the most practical, well-
qualified and efficient people with a kind of stupor. Time
and again these people from BOAC and the Ministry of
Supply and the rest of them must have got into trains at
London, saying purposefully: ' Now let's get this Brabazon
affair straightened out, once and for all.' As Surrey or
Berkshire rattles by in the pale sunshine one imagines them
opening bulging black brief-cases, looking over estimates
and specifications for a final check.

Purposeful and unromantic, they step out into the soft
country air. Already they hear low, Circean voices, but
they resist firmly, with some opening gambit about opti-
mum payload.

But it is no good. The moment they actually see the
great framework, they hear in their heads the sound that is
always associated in films with attacks of amnesia – a kind
of *bloy-oy-oy-oynggg* in a rising scale. Their vision swims,

their careful figures dance mazily about, they are wrapped about with twangling music. In no time they, too, are murmuring: ' *Ah, when will it be finished. Brabazon, Brabazon, tropical test, boats, balmy brabazon, for ever rest our oars, aerial navies, grappling in the blue, brababoats, whereabouts, hereabouts, brabzzz, bzzz . . .* '

NICHTAUS!

It is no accident that, while the English have exported soccer to almost the entire non-American world, including Scotland and Russia, their dreamy, green-and-white summer game has never had so universal an appeal, even at home. It may be only an minority even of Englishmen who do not regard the summer as a boring, dusty time between two football seasons, full of hot, empty Saturday afternoons with children endlessly demanding ice-cream. This is because soccer is more obvious and elemental, a simple formalisation of tribal warfare, of battle cries in the sharp, youthful air. But cricket involves contemplation as well as action.

The fleeting northern summer, though Amaryllis

daunce in greene, is subject to the wreckful siege of batter-
ing days, it is more real in the evocation of our poets than
it is in reality. By all means let soccer be played under the
harsh, obvious Mediterranean sun, on sandy grounds in
India, in Bolivia; cricket is bounded by great trees and
telephone wires, in which the gentlest summer breeze
presages autumn gales and winter ruin. At any moment a
cold wind may spring up, the wives in deck chairs will put
on their coats.

Although in many ways the quintessence of Anglo-
Saxonness, cricket is best understood when we remember
the old Western tales of sunset lands, of the heavy, doomed
Cornish summer of Tristan. It is an aesthetic strength, not
a weakness, of cricket that Rain often Stops Play, whereas
hardly any thing stops soccer. Soccer could never prompt
anything like the well-known lines of Francis Thompson:

> For the field is full of shades as I near the shadowy coast,
> And a ghostly batsman plays to the bowling of a ghost;
> And I look through my tears on a soundless clapping host
> As the run-stealers flicker to and fro, to and fro:—
> O my Hornby and my Barlow long ago!

Any sincere attempt, therefore, to translate cricket into
a foreign context commands our curious and attentive
respect. Now, by far the most serious attempt I have ever
seen is in an article called *Cricket, das Englische Nationalspiel*,
which appeared some time ago in a Swiss paper; and
attentive respect is what I have been giving it ever since.

This article was written by someone who clearly knows
England, and is aware that cricket is our *ausgesprochenes
Sommerspiel*, our out-spoken-about summer game, and that
ein guter Cricketspieler is as famous as *ein grosser Politiker*. But
it is no good. The very title sets us thinking of preposterous games by Tyroleans, under the great Alps, with

harsh cries of ' *Wie ist das?* ' and ' *Nicht aus!* ' mingling with the yodelling and the cowbells.

The stern German language gives the gentle terms of the game a brutal ,military force. The bat is the *Schlagholz*, or Beating-wood. The game is played on a *Rasenplatz*, a shaved or level place, like the parade ground at Potsdam, between the *Werfermannschaft*, the Throwing-man-company, and the *Schläger-partei*, or Beating-party. The latter leaves *nur zwei Leute*, only two people, in the *Feld*, the other nine remaining outside the *Spielplatz*, *gewissermassen in Picketstellung*. I should like to think that this means playing guessing games behind the picket fence, but I doubt it.

As might be expected, the German is at its best when describing sharp, climacteric moments in the game. One can be out *wenn ein richtig geworfener Ball das ' wicket ' berührt*, when a rightly thrown Ball ' *berührt* ' the wicket. What an admirable word this for the fatal crash the batsman hears behind him. All is over, his wicket is be-ruined.

There are many other details of the way in which one can be out, as when one brings *seinen Körper zwischen den weggeworfenen Ball und das Tor*, one's Body between the way-thrown Ball and, most curiously, the Gate, or Arch. Above all, one can be out *wenn er sich ' unfair ' benimmt*. ' Unfair ' is evidently untranslatable.

The author is perhaps more generous in describing the thoroughness with which cricket is taught in England than correspondents to ' The Times ' would admit. *In der Schule*, he writes, man learns *Geschicklichkeit, Genauigkeit, Schnell-igkeit und Reaktionsfahigkeit*. Well, I can remember being taught, not very successfully, the last two – speed and quickness of reaction. I don't think one could be *taught* a native quality like *Genauigkeit*, which I take to be a kind of cunning Knowingness. And as for *Geschicklichkeit*, I find it very consoling to learn that we are acquiring *that*.

Sometimes, on the green grass, under the heavy July cumulus lazily troubled by rumbling aeroplanes, surrounded by cottages and ladies making tea, we feel uneasily that we are fiddling while Rome burns. It is somehow reassuring to learn that all the time we are becoming *schick*.

THE SHIP'S DAMP PIPE

One of the most insuperable of literary problems must surely be the composition of directions for emergencies, such as drowning or fire. For there is bound to be a contradiction between the urgency of the crackling building, or the cry from the lake, and the calm, logical paragraphs of small print, numbered like notes on a biology lecture, which are found in parks and office corridors and ship's cabins. Indeed, the only attempt at realistic terseness that I have seen is in the Army notice, to be found in orderly rooms, among the trestle tables and cups of cold tea.

As I remember, this says, in large red letters 'Instructions in case of FIRE. I Shout FIRE! 2 Attempt to put it out. 3 Summon assistance. The number of the local Fire Brigade is . . . . ' It is pleasant to think of the soldier proceeding to some high tower in the barracks and calling out 'FIRE' in a high voice like the muezzin, before ' methodically attempting to put it out.'

Civilian instructions, by contrast, are incurably long-winded. In Hyde Park, for instance, there is by the Serpentine a curious shut-up building, like a small abandoned town hall, with a notice saying 'Royal Life Saving Society.' Nearby, there is a notice about drowning and artificial respiration which must run to about 3,000 words. In typography and layout it is similar to those printed sheets dealing with another emergency, The Treatment of Electric Shock, which one always sees in garages. Victim and reviver both have heavy black moustaches and bowler hats.

One feels that if an alarm *was* sounded in Hyde Park nothing at all would happen for about ten minutes, and then a posse of stalwart, moustachioed men in tight-fitting black costumes, like ballet practice dress, would appear round the corner at a brisk trot, dragging a sort of wooden platform on cartwheels, festooned with big coils of thin rope. An order would be rapped out, and numbers one and two would drop smartly to one knee . . .

The effect of textbook remoteness is greatly heightened when the instructions are in a foreign language. Recently I was reading the German lifejacket direction on the boat to Holland. The *Notsignal,* or Need Signal, is *einem langen Stoss der Schiffsdampfeifer – one* long blow on the Ship's Damp Pipe. When this signal is given, it says, then shall each Passenger put on a *Schwimveste,* or swim-vest. This is presumably in addition to the life-jacket, which is clearly indicated by another word, *Jacke.* Thus:

> *Halte die Jacke über den Kopf, stecke die Arme durch die Armlöcher. Sie wird leichter über den Kopf gleiten wenn die hohle Form der Ruckseite zuerst gegen den Nacken gehalten und die Vordenseite dann über den Kopf nach unter gezogen wird.*

Hold the jacket over the head, stick the arms through the armlocks. You are going to glide it more lightly over the head if the whole form of the rucksack is first held against the neck and the forward side is then yoked over the head from underneath.

It is extraordinary difficult to visualise these complicated manoeuvres. Can it be that there is a special form of life-jacket in Germany, a huge affair full of straps, like field service marching order, including a rucksack for iron rations, and these armlocks, which the people have been drilled to use from early youth? Possibly this unique apparatus is a relic of German abstention, in Hitler's time, from some Geneva conference about the standardisation of lifejackets.

One cannot help feeling that it is an abstention dearly paid for, and bitterly regretted, by the Germans themselves, as they hastily change, down below, into swim-vests, and fumble cursingly with armlocks, and yoke the forward side over the head from underneath, while the cabin tilts and fills with water and the frivolous English and French (there are, strangely enough, no Dutch instructions) leap lightly over the side. Perhaps the Dutch, a practical people full of natural *savoir-faire*, don't need any instructions. Perhaps they just *know*, and are later found calmly waiting to give artificial respiration to these Germans, shivering in their swim-vests and half strangled with sodden canvas. One hopes so.

THE SWAGERS

Practically the only wrong thing that Belloc ever said was that the Midlands are sodden and unkind. It is true that Birmingham is unpleasant when it is raining, but so is the Stockwell Road; so, for that matter, is Eastbourne.

When it's raining in the Midlands you know that the people are nevertheless having a jolly time in lighted interiors, in big warm dance halls, among the secret badinage of queues in fish-and-chip shops. When it's raining in places like Eastbourne there is nothing but the mouldering lounge, the paper fan in the grate, and what Louis MacNeice called ' the inter-ripple and resonance of years of dinner gongs.' No, the special mark of the Midlands is not wetness but *mystery*.

Nobody knows anything about Midlanders. The

Midland accent is the hardest to imitate. When the BBC
do a play with a Midlands character in it, the young
gentleman always obliges with something nearer to
Huddersfield than anywhere else.

There are nationally known comics who are Cockneys
and North Country men, but the only great Midland
comic was the late lamented Sid Field, and he was a
genius, an exception. There are funny Irish, Scots, Welsh,
Geordie, Liverpool and Zummezet stories, but none from
the Midlands. Midlanders are craftsmen, who speak only
with their hands. They form the mysterious heart of a
manufacturing country.

Now no Midland town is more mysterious, more central
and heartlike, than Coventry, which is where the north
and the south of England meet. From Coventry the road
northwards to Leicester goes through country that is
already beginning to look bleak and moor-like, and the
road south to Kenilworth goes under soft trees to the
mellow barns of the Shakespeare country and thence to the
melting Cotswolds.

Coventry is full of mysterious people who live in hostels
and make aeroplanes. Coventry has the mysterious legend
of Lady Godiva, with those curious stolid crowds, and the
mysterious far-off Coventry Carol, that sad lament at
Herod's cruelty. In the centre of Coventry, in St. Mary's
Hall, is an archaic, mysterious wooden figure that was
once a whipping-post. And on the outskirts there is a
large, modern-looking building outside which it says:
COVENTRY SWAGING COMPANY.

This seems to me the most mysterious activity I have
ever heard of. It seems impossible that there should be an
actual operation called swaging. ' Give it a dip in the
swaging tank, Bill.' ' Real, pre-war swaging on this job,

Fred.' 'J. Harris, 3, Railway Cottages, a swager, was summoned for driving a motor-cycle without a licence . . .' No, it doesn't ring true.

I am sure the Coventry Swaging Company is something far more archetypal, nearer to the mole-like, inarticulate Saxon heart of England. It is the Saxon craftsman's equivalent of the Vestal fire. Research would probably show that in the eighteenth and seventeenth centuries it was the Coventry Asswaging Company, and that it has, right from the dim past, been assuaging or propitiating some nameless deity. Inside this factory will be found no humming machines but a host of men and boys, seen dimly through a green smoke, going through balletic motions, endlessly raising their arms in formal gestures to an obscure Saxon god of activity and making. And yet, at the same time, silent. A factory that makes nothing. Swaging is the apotheosis of mechanical rhythm, a compound of forging, swinging and swaying.

But full details will never be known. It is no good historians looking in the Coventry Leet Book, that mine of medieval information, for accounts of the Couentre Swagynge Gild. Let them not expect to find, in any annals, entries such as *Paid Thos. Ford 4d., ale for ye Swagers*. For this is something at the heart of England, something that must not be spoken of. What it is that swagers do, how they are initiated and trained, is less likely to have been committed to writing than the most secret free-mason ritual.

Let us, therefore, driving past this factory in one of the fruits of Coventry's labour, not look in, or ask, or even wonder too much. Let us go back to London, or Bath, or York, knowing with a quiet heart that in the secret Midlands there is this transcendental blacksmith's shop, this secret earthy strength to which we return darkly when the bright, clear thoughts of southern, Roman logic have failed to satisfy our full natures.

Let us remember that being ' sent to Coventry ' dates from the unwelcome experiences of Cavalier prisoners in Parliamentary Coventry. There could be no possible communication between Cavaliers and Swagers. It is only now, after the rude strife of centuries, that the industrial State is begging to absorb them both into a unity. And this is a mystery which begins in Coventry.

BIG BORE

Surely Marx, or Lenin, or whoever it was, would have been nearer the mark if he had said that motoring, not religion, is the opium of the people. It is true that a car or a motor-cycle, standing outside the house, pregnant with god-like speed, the body that carries a soul over the high places and wooded valleys of England, or out to the vast nothing of the sea, gives its owner a genuine sense of liberation. It is true that the sound of second gears whining up summer hills is a valid modern symbol of escape and happiness, a sound which, heard in a city street, may be as evocative as a whiff of heather. But most people, in car or bus, have at some time recognised a second, purely compulsive element. In the words of MacNeice:

Man's heart expands to tinker with his car,
For this is Sunday morning, Fate's great bazaar,
Regard these means as ends, concentrate on this Now,
And you may grow to music, or drive beyond Hindhead anyhow,
Take corners on two wheels until you go so fast,
That you can clutch a fringe or two of the windy past.

Motoring in this sense is escape from ennui, as may very
easily be seen in garages. We stand in the oily sunlight
between rows of other people's cars, in this utterly silent
place. The two glass-partitioned offices, their doors open,
are empty. No-one comes. We cannot whistle on our
fingers, so we shout, something foolish like HOY, or
HELLO, or even I SAY THERE. And suddenly we realise,
alone, that we are still earthbound, that we cannot escape.
It is not until we are bowling along again that we forget.

Now ordinary cars, the kind shown in advertisements
with four smiling people inside, calmly rushing up steep
hills, are for those who are blissfully untroubled by this
knowledge that ennui lies behind earthly joy. This is the
tragic privilege of the aristocrat, the Stoic; and it is only to
be properly appreciated by people in Rolls-Royces or
Bentleys. I have always suspected this, but recently I saw it
conclusively confirmed in an advertisement in *The Times*,
by ' the largest official retailers of Rolls-Royce and
Bentley.' It said:

> We offer the finest selection of used post-war Bentleys in
> the United Kingdom and we can supply from stock at the
> following prices:

1947	..	..	..	..	from £2,350
1948	..	..	..	..	from £2,550
1949	..	..	..	..	from £2,850
1950	..	..	..	..	from £3,250
1951	..	..	..	..	from £3,750
1952 (big bore)	..	..	..	..	from £4,750

Does not this put openly into words what we have always thought about Rolls-Royces and Bentleys? Long before other cars achieved any sophistication these machines had already successfully hidden, indeed transcended, the mere vulgar mechanics of locomotion. One was never conscious of the *engine*, particularly in a Rolls-Royce. It never went wrong. Behind that radiator, shaped like the pediment of a Greek temple, was a sort of disdainful intelligence, almost a contempt for mere motion. And this was combined with a sort of *raptness*.

If you've *got* to move, said the Rolls-Royce, I can do it, at ninety miles an hour if necessary. But the chief thing is civilisation, contemplation. Come, sit on these fawn seats, behind this mahogany and plate glass. Let us (a maximum of three of us) discuss the Renaissance in Italy over some dry sherry while the boring fields go past. One of the consolations of life in post-war Britain was reading that Colonel McCormick, who owns the *Chicago Tribune* and hates Britain, none the less has a Rolls-Royce.

So with the Bentleys. From this splendid, this supremely philosophical advertisement, it is clear that we have scaled the ultimate height when we have languidly signed a cheque for £4,750 for our 1952 Bentley. We have been through what Christian mystics call the Purgative Way, and the Hindus *Pravritti Marga*, the path of Desire. We realise that it is all just a big bore.

Looking back to 1947, to that day when we tried to sound casual as we told the barman that we had just got a rather nice Bentley for £2,350, we see that we had a lot to learn. We rolled the hood back, we drove ostentatiously to the Derby, we took our friends and boastfully gave them champagne picnics; it all seems so *naïve*. In 1948 we bought an enclosed saloon. We were more retiring, we *thought* more. But we took it to Venice and Florence. We looked at cathedrals. In the 1949 model we sat on the lonely cushions, reading Plato and Plotinus, only turning on the magnificent radio for Bach. In 1950 we never turned the radio on at all, although it could get Bangkok. And so on, till 1952, when we just sit, silent, in the silent vehicle . . .

ANNUAL LAMPS

Life in a modern city, full of chance sights and associations blown away into infinity before their implications can be grasped, is like music, which can never be halted and fully examined at any particular point. We walk down the street, and a van passes bearing the extraordinary legend ' C. S. Rolls and Co., Guillotine Knife Grinders, 2-4, Bleeding Heart Yard.' Before we have time to imagine this appalling shambles we see a shop full of garden furniture; we wonder who on earth has so much money that he can spare £80 for a chintz-covered settee suspended in a kind of derrick.

Eighty pounds! It would take five men half an hour to erect this thing, pinching their thumbs and cursing, and by that time, in England, it would be raining, and – but here comes a fire engine.

There is a further musical parallel for this multiplicity.

In the basic community of Plato's *Republic* there are at first
only the husbandmen, the builders, the tailors, and the
shoemakers; merchants come later. So, too, there were
in the beginning the Greek modes, and later, in the
eighteenth century, the diatonic scale, precise and limited.
But now there is atonalism, where everything merges into
everything else – just as, walking through London, we are
aware of infinite gradations of commercial activity going
on in little offices and workshops, up flights of uncarpeted
wooden stairs, where typewriters tap behind closed doors:
a network of voices, bells and voices, murmuring or harsh,
all indirectly having to do with us, changing our lives – a
shadow-real activity endlessly filling the air above our
heads, on second and third floors.

Let us attempt the impossible for a minute, let us stop
the record of this vast music; let us examine two of these
activities. Let us consider the writing I saw last week on
two windows facing each other in a street near Tottenham
Court Road; *Annual Lamp Company*, and *Glass Benders*.

These seem to represent a complexity beyond which
civilisation can advance no further. What extraordinary,
un-guessed at need do they satisfy? Annual lamps. At first
sight the mind boggles, there seems no connection whatever between these amazingly disparate words. We might
as well have seen, on these windows, ' Pantomime Crank-
shaft Company,' ' Mousetrap Wind Bros.,' ' Egg Navigation Consultants,' or ' Straw Pianos, Ltd.,' Do they
make a tremendously ornate lamp, like the hat of Edward
Lear's Quangle Wangle

> . . . *with ribbons and bibbons on every side*
> *And bells, and buttons, and loops, and lace*

– a lamp so complicated that it takes a year to make? Is it,
perhaps, a huge lighthouse lamp, with parabolic reflectors,

big enough to have a bathroom inside, like that organ at Atlantic City?

But the very size of the modest premises belies these monstrous conjectures. Come, let us be more practical, more prosaic. It exists, this annual lamp. People gain their livelihoods by it. Perhaps there is an ordinary lamp factory, but it changes its directors every year, electing them from among the workers – a cross between the Co-op. and the John Lewis partnership. Perhaps it is a kiddies' novelty lamp, to enable them to read their Christmas annuals under the bed-clothes. Perhaps it is fairy lights for Christmas trees, or simply a lamp guaranteed to last one year . . .

But no, all these pictures dissolve as soon as we examine them closely. So, too, do our notions of the glass benders, holding their breath as a tiny increase of pressure is applied, then relaxing as they hear the familiar sharp cracking sound, sweeping the fragments of glass off the floor and putting them in a vat, to start all over again.

Wait a minute, though. Could there possibly be any connection between the two? Could it be that, one November afternoon, as the needle on the gauge mounts higher and higher, the glass does *not* crack? Significant glances are exchanged, like those of the masked surgeons in screen operations, until finally the glass is bent right round, in a perfect cylinder.

Yes, see them proudly carrying it across the road to the Annual Lamp Co. ' H'm, thought you'd never make it this year,' grunts the Lampmaster, ' still, it's a beautiful job. Now we can get on with our lamp. Well, see you next year. Let's have your invoice, won't you? ' And the deputation goes back, walking through the silent-roaring traffic, back up the wooden stairs into the formless tide of music, into the undreamable dream of the infinite city.

SMALL STRIKE

If some international body concerned with group attitudes,
such as Unesco, were to investigate the psychology of newspaper reading I am sure it would recommend revolu-
tionary changes. For it would discover that the eye of even
the most conscientious citizen, eager for a responsible
democrat's knowledge of world affairs, is always first
attracted by the little paragraphs at the bottom. Readers
of one of the London evening papers, for instance, probably
have just as clear a picture of the Tottenham Woman,
daily credited with a three-line saying in some police court,
as they have of Malenkov or Dulles. The Tottenham
Woman – a massive, Henry Moore-ish figure, monolithic,
ancient as the Piltdown Man, uttering, from among the
trivial people caught with no rear light, sibylline
aphorisms such as 'marriage cannot be mended like

boots.'

Perhaps Unesco would recommend that every day the lead story be about the Tottenham Woman, with the latest news from Berlin and Trieste in intriguing small paragraphs, thus:

NOT L-IKE-LY

The chances of a world war are not great to-day.

Eisenhower at New York.

It follows that in the most serious newspaper of all, ' The Times,' the interest of these small items is correspondingly greater. At the moment, I am ashamed to say, I am still thinking not about Senator McCarthy or the frontier incidents but this story:

PICTURES AND BOOKS
MISSING

Fifty pictures and 450 valuable books consigned by rail from London to Blackpool libraries and art gallery last week are missing, Mr. F. E. Cronshaw, chief librarian and curator, disclosed yesterday. They were intended for an exhibition to be opened on Saturday at the Grundy Gallery.

The Picasso lithograph ' The Dove,' dispatched by the Arts Council on Tuesday of last week, is also missing. It was thought last night that both consignments might have been delayed by a small rail strike and by the Whitsun holiday.

This seems far more interesting than the main story, ' British counter-action in Berlin.' We imagine elegant creatures from the Arts Council, with beards and silver-headed canes, picking their way delicately across a maze of railway tracks to complain at some gloomy headquarters, wringing their hands over the lost Picasso. But instead of an immensely practical railway official, showing them to brown leather arm-chairs, offering them railway tea, briskly consulting a wall-map with flags on it saying, ' Art Treasures in Transit as at 31 May,' they meet someone as vague and poetic as themselves. ' Ah yes,' he says, ' a lovely piece. The classic Mediterranean bird, the living rhythm of flight caught in reposeful peace by a tragic draughtsman. I shouldn't worry, gentlemen, I expect there's a small strike somewhere.'

A *small* strike. Do we not wish to know more about this, as about the Tottenham Woman? There is an elusive, Chekhovian quality about this paragraph, as though it should really end ' . . . . . *or* by the Whitsun holiday. Who knows? ' A connection is half hinted between the timelessness of art and the ceaseless effort of the railways to forget that their timetables and their parallel lines, laid across the shimmering, insect-humming fields in the silence of noonday, are a hopeless attempt to escape from ennui, a symbol of our lost ability to sit in one place and *live*. This is not a vast strike of engine-drivers or porters, but of the staff at some country junction, bored by the endless ting-ting of signal bells in their empty fields. It has become too much for them. They have stopped a train, and at this moment they are lying about in the signal cabin and the blackmouthed shed incongruously backed by waving elms, reading these valuable old books, musing on Picasso's glimpse of the eternal certainties. ' Listen to this, Fred. *There are also idols formed by the intercourse and association of men with each other, which I call Idols of the Market Place . . .* '

The telephone rings. A signalman tears himself away from a beautiful edition of ' Polyolbion.' ' Yes,' he says testily. A distant superintendent's voice, crackling with fury, asks why the 11.4 to Liverpool is held up. The signalman sighs ' Will they be any happier when they *get* to Liverpool? ' Resignedly he pulls a lever, and presently the train is heard approaching.

And who should get out of it but that official and the Arts Council party? Delighted to find the Picasso unharmed, they are also charmed by the signal box. ' So functional, a working model of Causality ' says an expert in Persian poetry. ' It does make one feel like King Carol, doesn't it, or whoever that monarch was that always rode on the fireplate. Have you any fireplates here? I tell you what, why don't *you* take all this stuff up to Blackpool, and we'll look after the signal box for you? . . . '

Actually, next day it said that the books were sent by road. But ah, signalmen! Ah, strikers! Ah, Tottenham Woman!

HOUSE OF REPUTE

It is easy to dismiss house agents as parasites, non-productive elements of a spent civilisation, commissionaires on the doorstep of the newly-wed's life, with palms discreetly held upwards for their ten per cent. But anyone who has wandered round with them in an endless dream of cream-painted doors, standing briefly in triangular rooms containing one dusty teacup, marvelling at what kind of domestic life could have gone on in those strange top rooms, like village halls, with rafters, must eventually think otherwise.

England, covered with houses, like a vast game of Monopoly played by godlike mathematicians, is an infinity of building which by now has lost all direct causal connections with the confused, far-off crowd of Victorian builders who made it. This masonry has accumulated a brooding, unknown life of its own. No Domesday Book could record the endless permutations of dark L-shaped halls, of steps into bathrooms, of curious-woven plumbing. It is therefore reassuring to feel that house agents, with their formal vocabularies, their refusal to be scared, are maintaining some sort of representation for the human race among all these houses, like an old gardener in an overgrown wilderness.

Only now and again do house agents lift the veil and show that they, too, have imagination, that they do not always look on cultured cities as a mere aggregate of mod. cons. – that they too, pushing a gloomy bush aside with an umbrella to show the excellent drains, know in their hearts that:

> . . . *the leaves were full of children*
> *Hidden excitedly, containing laughter.*

Here is a newspaper advertisement which appeared recently:

SUIT DOCTOR OR DIPLOMAT £6,950, 80 years. Fine PERIOD CORNER RESIDENCE, in private road; five perfect bedrooms, two superb reception, study, admirable offices; central heating radiator; garden; large modern garage; genteel sub-letting permitted: licence to practice psychiatry. A potential gold-mine..

This takes us, literally, behind the façade. What a fascinating, complicated household this is, after the calm, simple, prosperous days of the original Period, when carriages drew up in the private road and there was a sound of music in the superb reception rooms, while children stole down from the nursery, past the five perfect bedrooms, to peep through the banisters at the gay scene below!

What are the feelings of old residents in the road, when the black, closed car draws up and the bearded man,

obviously a doctor or diplomat, quietly disappears inside?
If he is a diplomat, why on earth does he want a place
licensed for psychiatry?

Let us ask Mrs. Carruthers de Vere, who has just taken a
bed-sitting room, with meals optional, there. ' My dear,
there's something queer going on in the house. The other
morning Miss Poole and I and that nice Mr. Fanshawe,
the one that used to be in Kenya, were having breakfast
when we heard the most terrible row coming from Dr.
Ludwig's study. Really, he has the oddest callers. This
time it was a little mousey girl whom I'd met on the stairs
once before, and she told me that she was the Empress
Eugenie. Well, we suddenly heard her shout *No! No! I tell
you Karl never gave me the plans. Let me go, you deviationist!* And
just afterwards I happened to look out of the window and
there was that awful foreign chauffeur, signalling with flags
to a *helicopter*. I caught his eye and he gave me the most *evil*
look. Then Mr. Fanshawe got up and rushed out, and we
haven't seen him or the mousey girl since . . . '

Or is this picture of a sinister, Raymond Chandlerish
nursing home wrong? Can it be that the genteel tenants
practise psychiatry themselves, interrupting the flow of
self-revelation from the couch to make a pot of tea on the
gas-ring. It seems unlikely. ' Really, Mr. Hawkins, do I
understand you to say you wanted to marry your *mother*
when you were eighteen months old? '

Besides, where would this diplomat entertain his guests,
arriving with monocles and tiaras, if the whole place was cut
up into a honeycomb of rooms for genteel psychiatrists? It
would have to be a wonderful house to make this sort of
thing possible. But then, as the agents know, all houses are
wonderful.

SIXTY MOTTLED BATH MATS

Although Malthusian reports on the increase of population and the urbanisation of farm-land keep coming out, no-one seems to have remarked on another serious menace – the extraordinary increase in the number of *things* since the beginning of the nineteenth century. For 150 years more and more people have been turning out an ever-increasing stream of boot-trees, alloy tubing, gongs, sponges, traversing head millers, pianos, lead gnomes, tarpaulins, crucibles, helical and volute springs, shawls, railway carriages, grommets, tricycles, pentode valves, sheds, lifebouys, Avometers, oil seals, templates, meshcranks, swishpins, and dashpots – the whole lot smelling now slightly fusty, like old curtains in a cupboard.

Not only is there going to be less room for people, if we go on like this. More and more of the people that *are* left will have to be secondhand dealers and auctioneers. Otherwise London will be buried under soft mounds of shawls and riding habits and cushions; the streets will be choked with armchairs, the fields littered with nests of tables, vases, skates and bicycles. Already we have entire districts, like Kensington Church Street, given over to this magical business of rescuing the debris of centuries from being a mere dead-weight collection of objects, bringing it back into the flux of life. Let us now consider auctioneers, who do this essential work not only for private, consumer goods but also for the vast output of the manufacturing under-world, of sad little factories that set out to make buttons or mugs or egg-whisks and then go bankrupt.

I have just been looking at the catalogue of a single day's sale by one of these big auctioneers. There are 959 lots, and the extraordinary crowd who gathered in the saleroom that day must presumably have been interested in every-thing from ' one universal belt lacer ' to ' two gross Trillo squeakers.'

Every effort is made to sort this vast second-hand cornucopia – this fruit of the ingenuity of craftsmen whose names are blown on the viewless wind, we know not where – into some sort of order. Thus there were doubtless solemn men with notebooks waiting for such items as ' 112 oak-veneered bow-drawer fronts ' or ' A chemical lavatory with pipes (as new) ' – or even ' sixty oval-shaped mottled bath mats.' But there must have been other, more exotic characters. We may imagine the eyes of the business men turned curiously on the gay but slightly faded couple who came for the ' Mayfair gramophone complete with key.' And these would get their own back when it came to

' Small tools in case.' ' In case of what? ' they would ask, giggling.

And then there is the section on Household Furniture, lost in this welter of small machines and clothes. The first four items, printed together as if to suggest they are all from one Household, were:

534 A small Buhl cabinet.
535 An Indian carpet (soiled, but unused, and in perfect condition).
536 A motorised wallpaper trimming machine (perfect).
537 A telescope and a hat stretcher.

What inconceivable Household was it that decided to sell these? Perhaps there was a man who, in his forties, suddenly became interested in gadgets but was married to a terribly house-proud woman, proud of her Indian carpet until the day when, laboriously trimming wall-paper by hand, he spilt a pot of paste on it.

' Well ' he would say, ' everybody knocks paste-pots over if they're long enough. This job takes too long with scissors. I know, I'll fix a little motor on them.' And he would devise this incredible machine, ordinary scissors on which a little popping motor sits, like the ones on the backs of bicycles. Rapidly he would paper the whole house, right up to the day when, papering even the attic, he discovers this telescope there. ' Why, Emily ' he would say, ' look how it extends. I believe I could modify this thing to make it stretch hats.'

We do not know. There is no time to consider . The over-whelming impression of the catalogue is *haste*, to get the stuff moving before London is choked and life comes to a standstill. Come, don't look so doubtful about the contents of Lot 548 – ' 18 lbs. women's heels,' or ' sack containing

wooden wheels '— or ' forty-eight pieces of assorted dolls'
parts (legs, arms and bodies).' Make up your mind, man.
And ' the lots are to be paid for to the auctioneer or his
representative and to be taken away with all faults, im-
perfections, and errors of description (' but look, I said
heels and you've given me these *wheels* ') at the puchaser's
expense and risk *before 5 p.m. on the day after the sale.*

Hurry, man – tomorrow we have to take in 500 feet of
alloy tubing, a marquee, a stuffed elephant, a double-
ended grinding spindle with three-phase Neco electric
motor, thirty padlocks with keys, two gross buster suits. . .

MONSTER JOKE BOMS

One of the most curious things about this century is the arbitrary line it draws between the serious and the comic. Humour is a vast industry on its own; and yet a great deal of solemn engineering skill is devoted to products which, though listed as serious, are fundamentally toys.

The real charm of television, for instance, is that it is a kind of super jack-in-the-box. And if anyone deny that motor-cars are toys, let him go to Shepherd's Bush and see them all milling round that triangular green where you turn off for Oxford. It is not difficult to visualise a low roof of wire gauze over the whole place, from which vertical rods at the backs of the cars strike bright blue sparks. Real cars are more like dodgems than dodgems are themselves.

The desire to avoid collision is more intense. The occupants of ' real ' cars have an even grimmer preoccupation with their circular motion, and the same anxious air of determined pleasure.

Out in the country, the frivolous cars whirl past the tolerant eyes of adult peasants. The chromium-plated arm things on the hoods of drop-head coupés are exactly the same as those on high-class prams.

Yet this is all a very serious business, with share-holders and steel allocations. And, by the same token, we tend to imagine that people who make officially comic things, such as indoor fireworks, Joke Boms that go THWUP in a tiny explosion of trinkets, spend the whole time chuckling. In fact I am sure it is the other way round. If the Joke List of a certain London shop is any criterion, it *is* the other way round, for this document is clearly the product of some very serious thought.

It comes in four Roneo'd sheets, of which the last three are short descriptions of the Jokes on Page 1. These include Plate Lifters (French make), Dehydrated Worms, Impossible Spoon Joke, Wobbly Match Box with Key, Joke Moustaches (6d.) Best Joke Moustaches (2s. 6d.) All Rubber Pencils, Bed Bugs Box (1s.) Stinky Scent Bottle (6d.) and Small Wireless Joke set in Match Box (1s.).

If you try mixing in a few serious items, from an advertisement in the ' Economist,' you will see what I mean about the arbitrary line: Impossible Spoon Joke, Babcock and Wilcox Watertube, Plate Lifters (French make), Plate Bending Rolls, Slotters ,Grinders, Platform Trolley and Bogey Hoppers, Joke Moustaches, Crushers and Disintegrators . . . . Does not this list read trippingly, as though all these things were made by the same firm? It is pleasant to imagine a merger, and the resultant production

of Impossible Babcock and Wilcox Watertubes and Joke
Bogey Hoppers.

When you get to the remaining three sheets it is rather
disappointing to find that they explain only the Jokes that
are obvious anyway, and even then the explanation is more
concerned with the effect of the Joke than its technical
details. Thus:

WOBBLEY CHEESE JOKE CAUSES roars of laughter.

BLACK BEETLE drop it in a friends drink.

DRIBBLE GLASS they cannot drink see them slobber.

STINKIE STINKERS push on in a cigarette causes horrible
smell.

PEA IN THE POT PUZZLE is to get the pea in the pot.

None of these Jokes really *needs* explaining. The Pea in
Pot puzzle particularly, is a perfect example of that funda-
mental difficulty of Definition which has led so many
thinkers into the belief that Philosophy is simply the problem of language. Indeed, it has about it a suggestion of
the ancient classical antinomies and problems, like the one
about the serpent eating itself. I don't think I shall buy the
Pea in Pot, for fear that my friends retire to the Cotswolds
and sit in a loincloth on a stone for twenty years to think it
out.

I would much prefer to have some of the obscurer Jokes
explained. I would like, for instance, to know what this
Small Wireless Joke is, and how it is set in the Match Box.
Is it a not very funny Joke, made in the early days at Savoy
Hill? Or is it a normal-sized, perfectly good joke, only
printed very small, so as to go into the Match Box? I would
like to know too, what Mr. and Mrs. Caudle (2s.) are, what
Seebackroscopes, Faciograph Chain Cards and Atomic
Shocking Letters are.

Most of all, if you drop Beetles in your friends' drinks, I

would like to know what you can do to your enemies. I would like to see a Joke List for them. *That* would be serious all right.

LOOK OUT FOR DWARFS

There are a lot of things we do not know about parks. We can never be quite sure whether we have won the battle against Nature, and these licensed survivals of the elemental in the middle of our stone cities, these places where we allow the grass to grow while fearing that some day it will come up between our paving-stones, inevitably stir in us drowned memories of earlier human attempts to rationalise the natural world. There is something Other than us in parks. At the lower end of the scale we recognise It in Its influence, like that of the moon, on people in their basic activities. City dwellers are attracted to courtship and murder in parks. We draw up codes, to limit and straiten the almost unimaginable activities to which the lawless, primitive flowers might urge us.

The more formal and urban the park, the wilder its by-laws assume its users will be. For instance, hidden away in those curiously un-Mayfair blocks of flats, all balconies and dustbins, behind Grosvenor Square, the authorities had the idea of making a little garden on the roof of an underground power station. You pass a door, from which warm, oily air comes, and there is a great cavern full of dynamos. You go up a few steps, and there, amazingly, is a place of stone flags, with shrubs in boxes, and a little fountain, and seats. Hardly anybody even knows about this place, yet it is extraordinary what the by-laws prohibit – ' games, brawling, fighting, quarrelling, gambling, betting, playing with cards or dice, singing, the practice of climbing the trees, railings or balustrade . . . ' No speech, address, performance, recitation or representation may be delivered . . . no vehicle of any kind is admitted.'

It is uncanny, almost as though there were, skulking about London, a nameless race of uncouth, lawless dwarfs, to whom the shrubs might well appear as trees to be climbed. No ordinary vehicle could possibly get up the steps to this place anyway, but Heaven knows what contraptions these trulls might drag up with them, as they range through the West End with high, squeaky cries, converging on Duke Street Gardens, intent on quarrelling and obscene recitations, finally brawling and fighting, pulling down the whole place like the dwarfs in *Peer Gynt*, so that the sterile, obedient, urban electricity can no longer be made below.

But that, as I say, is only the lower end of the scale. By-laws are the least direct of our dealings with the It of parks. Very much more direct are the curious buildings, half temple and half house, with which London parks, at any rate, are dotted. Anyone who has been past Hyde Park or Regent's Park on a bus will have noticed these little utility Parthenons, with lace curtains under Doric pillars. They are much too *low* for human occupancy, and besides, they have no doors that one can see. Very often there are no windows either – just a space filled in with yellow plaster. Who lives in them ? Surely they cannot but be the resorts of special park-demiurges, halfway between Pan and by-laws; gods who mend their own socks, but who, nevertheless, must be reckoned with; gods who are not seen . . .

But stay, perhaps they *can* be seen. For now I recall that, in the dark evenings, there are boards outside Hyde Park saying, astonishingly, ' Open at 5 a.m.' It is impossible to believe that real people want to go in parks at that hour. The only human explanation that one can think of, that it is for the convenience of the owners of very savage dogs which, during the day, would bite or drown the dogs of ordinary park-strollers, does not, on reflection, hold water, since the park would then obviously be *full* of savage dogs and noisy with battles to the death, at 5 a.m.

No, this is the hour so well described by Stevenson as that when all things ,men and the beasts in the fields, turn over in their sleep, when a *frisson* passes through the world; when dreams and reality meet in parks. At 5 a.m. in Hyde Park one might see, wafting from the solemn museums of Kensington or the Albert Hall, bearded geographers and mining engineers and oratorio composers, walking gravely under the trees to the music of Parry. In St. James' Park one might see a gay, Edwardian, sugar-candy-pink ballet of people in ' stage coaches, omnibuses, hearses, brakes and charabancs, entering the Park without the written consent of the Commissioners ; ' or perhaps a dour squad of mechanics, ' giving, or receiving instructions in managing or *repairing* (my italics) ' such vehicles.' And if one watched one of those little houses very carefully, one might see Something that really justified the effort of getting up so early.

MID YELL AND GOTT

It is quite extraordinary how modern science and technology, which everyone says are destroying time and the racial contemplation of old myths, are really unable to do more than scratch the surface of our ideas. Let us, for instance, contemplate the telephone exchanges of the Shetlands, which, at 9 a.m. on 2nd July, 1951, became a Group Centre in the Aberdeen Zone:

Baltasound	Gott	Scalloway
Bigton	Gutcher	Skellister
Bixter	Hamnavoe	Sullom
Brae	Haroldswick	Sumburgh
Bressay	Hillswick	Symbister
Bridge End (Shetland)	Lerwick	Uyeasound
Burravoe	Mid Yell	Vidlin
Cullivoe	Mossbank	Voe
Cunningsburgh	North Roe	Walls
Dunrossness	Reawick	Weisdale
Fairisle	Sandness	Westerskeld
Fetlar	Sandwick (Shetland)	West Sandwick

This list was printed for a purely organisational purpose, and it has purely technical footnotes, such as ' Under Aberdeen Zone and against Aberdeen Group Centre *delete* Lerwick in the Approved Automanual Switching Centre Column. *Add* Lerwick in Group Centre Column.' Yet how many people seeing for the first time this superb catalogue, like the synopsis for a saga, really think of black modern telephones shrilling in isolated farmhouses ? Is it not rather a marvellous evocation, in terse notes as pregnant as the jottings of Pascal, of what we all feel about the Shetlands, especially those of us who have never been there ?

For the Shetlands are quite different from the Hebrides, which are full of mysterious Celtic songs in soft curtains of rain, of pale queens with red hair, and kings with seven sons, in a soundless land behind the sunset. The Shetlands belong to the hard, bright, and above all, suprisingly sunlit lands of the north, where one expects everyone to be dressed in furs but finds instead pavement cafés and warm theatres and summer festivals; the gay, almost Mediterranean green copper spires of northern capitals.

There is something of the unexpected quality of the land in that northern fairy story about the little girl, ill treated by her step-mother, who fell into a well and found a strange bright country at the bottom, from which she returned with rich rewards for her kindness, and to which her envious step-sisters went with less success; a world at once naive and sophisticated, and curiously cosmopolitan.

Now this telephone list, with its cryptic suggestions, like runes on a half buried, timeworn stone, immediately suggests this kind of world to us. There is this Frenchman Bressay – Monsieur Felix Bressay, who teaches dancing at the palace. There is this Chaucerian figure of the Fetlar, singing his songs of far-off lands as he goes from house to house doing odd fettling jobs. There is the enchanted Fair Isle, to which the hero Haroldswick must attain despite the spells put on the evil waters of Uyeasound by his wicked brothers Gott and Gutcher; they bewitch him into the curious state of waking sleep known as dunrossness just as he is due to slay the dragon Sullom and rescue the Princess Voe from the fate that has already overtaken her sisters Burravoe, Cullivoe, and Hamnavoe . . .

Yet although some parts of this allegedly scientific list are far down in our ancestral northern memories, others are nearer the ordinary modern consciousness, so that the total effect is a wonderful integration of past and present, fact and fable. Thus, we are by no means limited to the conventional late medieval setting of ordinary fairy tales.

Other inhabitants of the country include the Dickensian cockney Vidlin – Joe Vidlin, an ostler; and there is even Walls the commercial traveller, known as Mid Yell because he is always surrounded by boon companions roaring with laughter at his jokes. These are semi-classical figures, like Harlequin or Mr. Bones the Butcher.

Then, nearer still to 'reality,' we have Baltasound, which is of course, an anagram for Basutoland; this brings us to the world of John Buchan, and the Calvinistic destiny of the Scots boy who observed the African King, Prester John, at his rites on a Scottish beach and later had adventure of him in the peacock lands.

Finally we come right into the everyday world with West Sandwick, clearly a perfectly ordinary place with a flagstaff and a golf course. And I happen to know there is an airport at Sumburgh. But, ah, the twangling music on Fair Isle. and the black waters of Uyeasound! There are no telephones *there*.

MAC'S HAEMOGLOBINOMETERS

One of the charms of a great city which has grown up organically, a charm that no abstract, planned city can possess, is the sense of place, of the *genius loci*. A fine example of this in London, as I have pointed out before, is Victoria Street.

To those who have the proper view of a city as the crown and flower of all human expression, both sacred and profane, it is no irreverence to say that Victoria Street, with its offices in tall Business Gothic, flows on quite naturally from Westminster Abbey, with the offices of the Ecclesiastical Commissioners forming a gentle and logical transition between the Church and Engineering. For Victoria Street, starting at No. 1 (Pre-Piling Surveys, Ltd.,) is the headquarters of firms who build bridges and pipelines all over the world.

Behind Victoria Street is Queen Anne's Gate, whence one can see the wireless masts of the Admiralty, doubtless in touch with sleek grey battleships. Whatever doubts assail our nineteenth-century imperial confidence, these engineers, having conferences with sunburnt men who have just driven direct from London Airport, look outwards across the seas, even while they sit in the shadow of the great Abbey.

Victoria Street contains not only firms but various *tabernacles* of engineering. Of these the most august, unnoticed by the hurrying thousands, is the British Standards Institute. But one morning recently I was not hurrying, so I went in. It is filled with people who do nothing else but draw up standards. Whether you make laminated safety glass, Haldane-type haemoglobinometers, nuts and bolts, tape and tung oil, or rennet and acid casein, there is a British standard to tell you what specifications it should pass.

Yet, so well is the national genius expressed in Victoria Street, the BSI is by no means a cold, abstract place, forever compiling a kind of Encyclopædia of hardware. There is none of the Continental abstract rationalism that one associates with the place at Meudon, near Paris, where there is a piece of platinum exactly one metre long, to which all the metres in the world must ultimately be referred. The BSI is warm and empirical· It has to do with us and we with it. It is concerned also with relating the precision of modern engineering science to our traditional culture. There are British Standards for women's clothing, and envelopes, and milk. Best of all, there is one (No. 1749, 1951) on Alphabetical Arrangement.

The co-operating organisations on this one range from the Bodleian Library to the Imperial Bureau of Soil

Science, with the result that the ' typical ' indexes they
give to illustrate word order look like real quotations from
the index of some vast book, uniting all knowledge on a
scale that we who only pass through Victoria Street, like
trippers in Oxford, can only guess at. Here are two
examples:

Mac goes to school	Saint-Amand, Mary
McAdam, E. D.	St. Clair, Robert
MacAlpin, Michael	Saint George and the Dragon
Macbeth	St. John, Robert
McCrystol, R. G.	Ste. Anne
Machinery	Saint-Beuve
Mackenzie, Compton	
M'Kenzie, John	
Macmillan, Norman	

To what kind of book could this be the index? What vast
sociological canvas is this, in which Compton Mackenzie
and Sainte-Beuve deck ugly black machinery with delicate
garlands of literature? My own guess is that it is a monster
study in the style of P E P, entitled *Edinburgh: A Study of the
Survival of Humanistic Culture in a Modern City.*

' Mac goes to school ' is the first chapter, in which we
have an exhaustive study of the curriculum in the elemen-
tary schools of Leith. Within earshot of the steam hammers
in the shipyards, the growing boy learns of great nineteenth
century engineers, like E. D. McAdam and Sir Michael
McAlpin. But at the same time he is attuned to an older,
wilder music, the old ,grim tales of Scotland, like Macbeth.

Later he meets R. G. McCrystol, a little old school-
master to whom generations of Edinburgh boys owe their
first glimpse of the glorious world of the imagination – the
sort of man who is little known but who, when he dies, gets
tributes from surprisingly famous people in ' The Times.'

As a young man Mac follows Compton Mackenzie, he

becomes a Romantic. Eagerly he reads everything he can find about the Forty-Five and the Auld Alliance. This makes him a Francophile which would account for all those French items; and this in turn leads him into wider European sympathies, to the study of Arthurian legend, of Froissart and Mallory, and thence finally to a sympathy even with England and her patron saint.

It is gratifying to feel that a man of such wide culture should not end up as a neurotic intellectual, but by selling machinery from an office in Victoria Street.

PLEASURE OF POSTS

In any Gallup Poll of the popularity of Government Departments the Post Office would surely come first – in July, let alone at Christmas. Even on the purely political plane the Postmaster-General always seems to be a moderate likeable character. One never sees any PMG reported as saying, at Haverfordwest at the week-end, that the Other Party has been squandering pillar-box paint.

One imagines that at party meetings, for a century or more, PMG's have sat silent and unhappy while their colleagues wrangled over tariffs or insurance or nationalisation, trying to get a word in edgeways about some charming idea such as murals in Post Offices, or greetings telegrams; being listened to perfunctorily, and escaping at last to the admirably named Mount Pleasant, among the white Ionic pillars and Temples of Love, where wing-sandalled Messengers flit airily to twangling heavenly music. Greetings telegrams! You'd never catch, say, the Income Tax people designing a gay Refund Form for the rare occasions when you have paid too much tax; and if *they* have a headquarters I expect it's called Mount Dreary.

The supreme example of the Post Office's urbanity is its ability to make even rules and regulations seem like light reading. The Post Office Guide is never reviewed, or recommended as a Christmas presemt. But it is compact of romance, poetry and, above all, humour. It is wryly aware both of our own domestic habits and of the extraordinary phobias nearly all foreign countries seem to have that we shall send them bees, arms or bulbs.

In the section on unsealed letters, which may carry ' conventional or formal messages,' the Guide points out that such words as ' arrived safely ' or ' see you Monday ' are not formal. And it knows all about rural life. ' A resident in a rural district ' it says, ' may call for letters at the proper delivery office in preference to delivery by postman, on payment of a fee of £1 10s. a year, irrespective of whether or not he uses a private bag.' How different from Chile, where it's the other way round and one pays the postman. This is crowded Britain; we see the Colonel, his private bag on the back of his bicycle, glancing triumphantly at the curtains from which a face has withdrawn just too late: *she'll* never see his mail again.

There is a fine impartiality too, as between North and South. Mail may re-directed ' during wakes or holidays.' There is a special note about sending chrysanthemums to Northern Ireland. And, in a wonderfully sporting paragraph, details are given of the distances from all London termini of the nearest express office; from Waterloo it is 825 yards. One would not be surprised to learn that there is a Post Office race over this course every Shrove Tuesday.

But it is the foreign section that really makes this admirable book. Who would have thought, for instance, that you cannot send *gooseberry bushes* to Holland? At what international postal conference did the Dutch delegate, his mind full of the awful ships converging on Rotterdam, their outlines blurred by huge deck cargoes of gooseberries, insist on this prohibition? Why does America, of all places, prohibit ' pictorial representations of prize-fights? ' And while it seems logical enough that the Vatican City should prohibit ' mechanical lighters and playing cards,' why should the Tonga or Friendly Islands be among the few that prohibit ' musical instruments and perfume? ' Can it be that they are sick of the lotus-eating life and fear that such gay imports will distract a naturally lazy and cheerful people from the new industries so painfully started – fruit canning, weaving?

Why on earth does all South Africa *except Basutoland* allow us to send eau-de-Cologne? Why is it always South American countries which are afraid we shall send them parcels of worn clothing without a certificate of de-infestation from a consular officer?

There is a marvellous awareness of that world, full of bright birds and dangerous rivers, which lies beyond the measured tread of civilised postmen. The Guide says pregnantly ' Insurance as far as Moshi, Songeya, Lushoto . . . ' After that our parcels, even if they do not contain ' ostrich feathers not made up,' are on their own.

We live in our brick built suburbs, leading calculable lives; but the Post Office knows our response to the call of strange lands, our commerce with Florianopolis, Fortaleza, Bimberéké, Grand Popo, and, magically, Afar (Mauritania).

CHRISTMAS BOX

When it comes to admiring people, I bet I go farther than
most men
In admiring postmen.
When Dr. Johnson met soldiers, he said he felt *smaller;*
Well, that's how I feel when I'm still in bed and along
comes this matutinal caller;
When I see postmen, carrying sacks, their frames all bent
It makes me consider how my life is spent.
Postmen wear modest uniforms, with red piping,
Modest is their demeanour; you never hear postmen
griping,
Postmen don't strike, they're too busy helping the nation.
Postmen are instruments of Communication;
Animals are good, but people are better
Because they can send their soul in a letter.
Oh Civilisation, think what a debt thou owest
To Postmen, getting up at four, when vitality is lowest,

Reporting at bleak, windy, banging, cheerless halls
Where vans come right inside, since there is a roof but no
walls,
Postmen don't seem to mind cold and rain, they seem
impervious,
They are the nicest people in the Civil Servious.
Most people want more and more
But Postmen go to heaven through a little door
Because in their youth they were telegraph boys with
bicycles
And now they are content to walk, among hail and icicles.
I always feel
That foreign Postmen – French ones, for instancea – ren't
quite real
They have draggly moustachios
And call in at cafés in a most unprofessional way, for
cognac and pistachios,
While in the States
They don't come properly to people's doors, they lazily
drop the mail in those dovecote things by the garden
gates –
And while we're considering postmen overseas,
The ones in India have four days' stubble, and take naps
under trees.
But *our* postmen are aboriginals, better than any,
I bet we *invented* Postmen, like railways and the Spinning
Jenny –

    You civil Civil Servants, know
    Your labours not unlauded go
    O hear my praise all loud and ardent
    You Postmen Absolute, Displayed, Regardant.

IN THE SWIM

No one enjoys more than I do
The pleasures of the swimming pool, or Lido
When I lie on the concrete bordering this municipal
moisture
The world is my oisture.
I do not talk, or read novels of detection,
No, what deep water produces in me is deep reflection;
I am one of the many chaps who
Have only to be at a swimming pool, and they start
thinking of the primordial ocean, which the Egyptians
called Nu and the Babylonians Apsu;
Water, says Jung, the sage of Switzerland,
Is an archetype of the Unconscious, from which our
Conscious, the part that fills in income tax forms, rises in
scattered peaks or bits o' land.

At swimming pools, when the weather is finer
I dream of broken aqueducts by ruined cities in Asia
Minor.
Surrounded by laughing bathers, I am as old as Tiresias or
Gerontius
I swim through a green and chlorinated Unconscious,
I love all men —
but what is this?
Two golden men and a golden miss
Seem to think they're admired by all
For their solemn game with a medicine ball;
They stand in poses we all have seen
On the covers of many a health magazine,
It's clear they think, from their graces and airs,
We wish we could all have bodies like theirs
Sooner or later they drop their catches,
The wet ball lands on my pipe and matches;
My dreams no longer hatch out from their eggs
When gymnasts trip on my outstretched legs.
The view I take of their sport is dim,
I crossly rise and dive in for a swim —
But here again I am far from solo,
I come up for air in a game of polo . . .
Too late! Too late! I was just a fool
To think I could dream at a swimming pool.

THE MUSIC'S THE THING

Ever since adolescence
I have loved music, though I have given up pianolescence,
As complaints got noisier and noisier, which
Is a fate clearly different from that of Moiseiwitsch.
No, when it comes to concertos
I am passive, not active; I listen to Dennis Matthews, who
    is always on his toes, or Nina Milkina, who is always on
                her toes.
I am a man who when he getteth an opportunity to listen,
            he seizeth that opportunity, he grabbeth
Particularly on the Sabbath.   –
Now, I have a complaint against the BBC, and this is its
                burthen
(It's my only complaint; they haven't got *feet* of clay, just
              one big toe is earthen) –

Why do they think that Sunday afternoon, when we are
                              all in a lovely stupor, or daze,
Is a good time for *plays*?
This is an hour when *je suis*, not when *je pense;*
If ever there was a time for music, this is it, *par excellence.*
I lie stranded on a warm beach of leisure,
I wish to be washed over by voluptuous waves of classical
                              music, rolling in majestic measure;
O BBC, I am replete with roast potatoes and the week's
                              meat ration,
Pray give me the sad or triumphant horns, the anguished
                              violins, the whole apparatus of music's passion.
On Sunday afternoon I dream, I am at my best,
I wish to hear heaven-and-hell Mozart, the Edwardian
                              sunset of Elgar, the harsh cries of Beethoven; I wish to
                              drink from deep wells of the West;
This is no time
For silly actors getting excited about some uninteresting
                              crime.
When I turn on the radio on Sunday afternoon and it's
                              only *talking*, I turn it off again in disgust.
If people have got to speak, if they must,
Let them speak
During the week . . .

> *The Sunday lunch, O splendid Corporation,*
> *Should not be spoiled by thought or cerebration;*
> *Please ponder on the fact that Orpheus*
> *Deliciously and aptly rhymes with Morpheus.*

THE RUG CRISIS
(BY A PERSIAN JOURNALIST)

All the newspapers I had read on the westward journey
to London had given no hope that Dr. Attlee would make
any deviation from his Government's plan, approved
unanimously by the Housecom last month, to take over
the Persian carpets in our Embassy at London and put
them in the Victoria and Albert Museum. We are now in
the second month of these angry and strained negotiations,
in which the long-dormant flame of English nationalism
has been fanned to a white heat. As our aircraft swooped
over the sprawling, disorderly slums of south London, it
looked just the same as in the days when I had known it
long ago, before the British rug crisis suddenly flared up
into a major threat to world peace. Under those grey roofs

live a people who for long ages have slumbered among the heavy mists of their Atlantic torpor, content to look dreamily upwards, their energies absorbed by centuries of in-breeding, their minds dulled by the ancient, un-changing ritual of *krikit*, so incomprehensible to the progressive, nationalistic young Eastern nations. But today these advanced Eastern ideas have come home to roost in this little known corner of the mysterious West. We cannot set back the clock, and it is clear that any solution of the rug dispute must take English nationalism into account.

After I had landed at the primitive, hutted airport, called Heathro ('heath' is a native word meaning a piece of wild, unkempt land) I did not have long to wait for signs of popular excitement. Lorry loads of students from Battersea Polytechnic and the National School of Bakery picketed the airport, chanting such slogans as 'Death to the rug-stealers' and 'Give the people their carpets.' It was only with the help of a surly police escort that we reached the twisting, quaint streets of the capital, where old-fashioned native taxis jostled American cars almost as sleek and new as the ones at home in Persia.

The same evening I managed to get to the Housecom to hear a statement made by the ailing Dr. Attlee, who had been carried there on a litter from the house in a remote street nearby where he is staying, instead of in the palatial premier's home in the country, because of the uneasy political conditions in England. Since the assassination attempt on Dr. Attlee's predecessor, Dr. Churchill, by a section of the extremist Women's Institutes, Dr. Attlee has been closely guarded. He is maintaining a desperate balance between at least four groups – the Kill-Them-All Party, led by Dr. Waldronsmithers, the Landowners' Party, led by Dr. Churchill, his own New Statesman Party,

and the secret Spiv Brotherhood. This latter is composed
of paid agitators, mostly from outlying provinces such as
Strangeways, Broadmoor, Winson Green and Dartmoor,
and no Eastern traveller is safe, very far from the capital,
from wandering Spiv gangs armed with clubs. Although
there is no clear proof, it is obvious that the Spiv party is
being financed by England's sinister northern neighbour
whose leader, Dr. Wendywood, is only too anxious to fish
in troubled waters and to revive the old Scottish dream of
world conquest.

In a passionate speech Dr. Attlee, who fainted twice,
defended the inalienable rights of the English people to the
' so-called Persian carpets.' He contrasted the luxury of the
Persian Embassy, which had enjoyed the traditional
hospitality and courtesy of the English people, with the
carpetless walls of the Victoria and Albert Museum before
the ' ever glorious nationalisation decree of March.' At one
point, when he praised Dr. Sirleigh-Ashton and Dr.
Gibbsmith and ' the heroic band of defenders of English
liberties in South Kensington ' the Housecom burst into
wild cheering.

Later I had an interview with an official at the Persian
Embassy where the loyal and devoted staff are staying on
in spite of great difficulties, working on cold, stone,
carpetless floors, although the temperature is sometimes
below zero. He told me about the delegation composed of
Embassy men and representatives of the Alsorhan Carpet
Company, makers of the disputed carpets, which was
received last week by Dr. Attlee. He took them on a tour
round cinemas and hotels with wretched carpets, or
coconut matting, and round great bare grammar schools
and even slum houses in Kensington where there were no
carpets at all. ' He accused us bitterly of selfishness, and

told us that our carpets belonged to the world,' my informant said, ' and since the carpets were on English soil he would rather they were thrown into the sea than that the Persians' high-handed claims for their private use should be satisfied.'

A member of the party asked how England would be able to clean the carpets, let alone renew them. ' We shall allow foreign visitors to the Victoria and Albert Musuem to enter at prices three per cent. below international rates,' replied Dr. Attlee. He also spoke vaguely of importing foreign carpet-cleaners from Italy. An Italian newspaper yesterday reported that Count Tomato, representing a big carpet-cleaning interest in Milan, had flown to Dr. Attlee's bedside, but official sources (or Italian sources anyway) promptly denied this. It has also been officially denied in Washington that an American firm has offered to invest ten billion dollars in the School of Carpet Technology at Kidderminster and to send carpet-weaving technicians.

Meanwhile, feeling in London is kept at fever pitch by daily demonstrations. At a mass meeting of the Kill-Them-All party, which is recruited mainly from the rural areas of Surrey, rugged farmers armed with scythes marched to the Persian Embassy uttering their war cry *Rhubarb, Rhubarb.* Yesterday students of London University upset trams on the Embankment, using crow-bars developed specially for this peculiarly western operation. The fiercely anti-Eastern *Daily Telegraph* (Englishmen take a naïve delight in the old-fashioned telegraph, superseded in more modern countries by the telephone) carried an editorial denouncing a sweet-manufacturing firm in Huntingdonshire for calling its product Turkish Delight instead of Huntingdon Pleasure.

Such is the picture of London today. It is easy for

Persians of the old-fashioned gunboat school to advocate sending a strong naval and military force, or economic sanctions, such as the withholding of Persian oil, which would have crippling effects on England's ambitious industrial programme. But such action would serve only to inflame the entire West. The Isle of Wight, for instance, which has always looked to the East for inspiration after gaining its independence with powerful Eastern help, is known to favour moderation in the present dispute. We must be patient and hope that when Dr. Gifford, the American ambassador to England, presents his plan, under which the carpets may be leased to the Victoria and Albert Museum for a period of 99 years on payment of 7s 6d, it may prove acceptable to both parties. Galling as this may be to Persian pride, it will not make much difference in the long run to our world-wide carpet supremacy. Dr. Attlee may not be the most reasonable of negotiators but, compared with Dr. Churchill and Dr. Waldronsmithers, he is a moderate. Any hasty action on our part may upset the whole delicate balance of Europe and consequently of world peace.

CLANGPAN'S COPY

People are always telling me confidential stories about famous authors who were once in advertising. ' Of course, you know So-and-so invented Night Starvation ' they say ... and So-and-so is always a different name.

I always smile in a superior way, not because I know who really invented Night Starvation, but because their stories fill me with nostalgia for the good old days at P B T F (Pendlebury, Bostock, Tinklepenny and Fudge) when the great Clangpan was in charge.

Clangpan was the only director I ever knew who really had good writers and gave them their head. I well remember the scheme we did for Puffmaster Steamrollers. ' Copywriting has got into a rut,' he boomed (or did he twitter? Funny how little details like that escape one over

the years). ' I don't want a lot of stuff about quality and
' *First again.' Puffmaster wins slow steamroller race at Lille
Rally.* I want something dynamic. The steamroller is
symbolic of the modern age, and yet it has a formal,
nineteenth-century beauty. I want writers who can say all
this with a fresh eye. I want you to get in touch with T. S.
Eliot, Noel Coward, Gertrude Stein, P. G. Wodehouse and
G. K. Chesterton, and we'll have a briefing meeting next
Thursday.'

I got busy. Gertrude Stein sent a telegram from Paris;
*steam roller steam roller steam roller steam roller steam yes yes
steam.* Shaw sent a postcard saying ' This is one of my
famous postcards but I'm not saying anything famous on it
because you didn't invite me . . . '

Ah, what a meeting that was! After Clangpan had
shown round the artwork (a composition called *Steamroller
and Guitar*, by Picasso) Noel Coward said ' One supposes
this machine is some sort of appliance for making steamed
jam roll in suburban kitchens. But how boring! '

' Not at all,' said G.K.C., ' the steam roller has a kind of
monstrous gay solidity. And have you noticed that the
faster the flywheel goes round the slower the roller goes?
That's the paradox of life . . . . the harder we work the less
ground we cover. The steam roller is like man; the wild
steam shut up in the heavy iron is like the wild soul of man,
caught up in his dull body . . . . '

' Ah, you writing gentlemen!' said Clangpan, ' you'll be
the death of me. Now, to business. I have asked you all to
come here because, frankly, I think that in Puffmaster we
have a theme worthy of you. Powerful and poetic, as Mr.
Chesterton has said. And yet, in its measured back-and-
forth movement having the limitations of tragedy . . . a
point for Mr. Eliot. Also, somehow comic ' (a bow to Mr.

Wodehouse); ' and mysterious mysterious alas backwards goody forwards, Miss Stein. Well, I think that's about all. We have until next Thursday.'

The company dispersed after a small banquet and cabaret in the directors' dining room. Less than a year later the copy started coming in. What a scheme it was. Here are some of the insertions. You can guess who wrote which, I hope.

> Before the District Council was, to whom our rates are owed,
> The rolling English engine made the rolling English road;
> A bumpy road, a pothole road, a road all dust and mire,
> Until the roller rolled it down as motorists require
> And made it all so smooth again, so kind to tyres and tread,
> That just for joy from Birmingham we drove to Beachy Head.

YES, MILLIONS OF LONDON HOUSEWIVES HAIL PUFFMASTER.

* * *

JULIA: Darling, let's get divorced.

PHILIP: Do you really mean it? I've always wanted to be your lover.

JULIA: (*Looking out of the window*) I say, they're making the road outside. I wonder how they got the steamroller round the mews corner.

PHILIP: They lowered it from a balloon.

JULIA: Pig.

PHILIP: Pig yourself.

JULIA: No, I mean how do they steer it?

PHILIP: They stop one wheel.

JULIA: Don't be silly. The boiler would burst. I bet they don't. I bet they turn the roller.

PHILIP: I tell you they stop one wheel. Like tractors.

JULIA: Tractors have caterpillars.

PHILIP: They stop one wheel.

JULIA: Bore. I'm going to ask the man.
(*Exit, Paula comes out of cupboard.*)

PAULA: I don't know what you ever saw in that woman.
Of course they stop one wheel.

PHILIP: Darling!
(*Enter Julia.*)

JULIA: I'm going to marry the steam roller man. He
lives in Streatham and he's an Ancient Buffalo.
And they *do* turn the roller, so there!

ALL: And Millions of London housewives hail Puffmaster!

* * *

Backwards and forwards
Only the cause and end of movement
Timeless, and undesiring. Sometimes I think
The steamroller does not move at all
Or only in the middle way.
Ridiculous the slow waste stones
Stretching before and after.

Ou est la plume de ma tante?
J'ai perdu mon chapeau
Ein zwei drei.

The funnel
Belches smoke
The shiny piston
Whirs in the quiet street.

O steamroller
Teach us to be crushed
YES, MILLIONS OF LONDON HOUSEWIVES HAIL
PUFFMASTER!

We were having a hair of the dog at the Drones Club when Bertie Wooster tottered in. ' I've bought a steam-roller,' he announced. ' I didn't mean to.' Alarming. The world was bad enough without this pitfall, if a chap could buy steamrollers without meaning it. I looked round uneasily to see if I'd got one, too. But I saw only the familiar fizzogs.

Bertie was explaining. ' I dodged into this place to avoid this female,' he said, ' and there were lots of rolls of lino-leum, and chaps in bowlers, and a chap at a desk shouting the odds. He sort of leered at me; I didn't want to be stand-offish, so I gave a sort of wan wink. And the chappie banged his gravel or whatever that thing is and yelled ' Sold to the gentleman over there. Lot 203. A *steamroller.*'

' Have you got it here?' said Reggie.

' Well, it's not far away yet.'

' What d'you mean?'

' Well, they made me drive it away—some law about having the stuff off the premises by 5 p.m. on day of sale—and they showed me how to start it. But I couldn't stop it, so when I got here I just jumped off. I expect it's got to Knightsbridge now . . . '

How we all exclaimed ' YES, MILLIONS OF LONDON HOUSEWIVES HAIL PUFFMASTER.'

* * *

steamroller steamroller steamroller
in the, yes,
on the grass, alas,
on the road, be blowed
words is steamroller
aplenty apuffa puffa
steamroller

PUFFMASTER HAIL HOUSEWIVES LONDON OF MILLIONS

ADVICE TO HUSBANDS

Spring-cleaning is a basic human experience. Faced in the right way, it sets the seal on married love. In these days, however, for many young couples it holds needless terrors. The strains and stresses of modern civilisation cause husbands to regard this beautiful, *natural* function with fear, sometimes with real horror. Instead of seeking advice from experts they fill their minds with half-digested stories of difficult cases. Older husbands, who ought to know better, seem to get a perverse pleasure from recounting ghoulish legends, most of them mere old husbands' tales. Many perfectly healthy young men have been frightened into a ' difficult ' experience by hearing of ' Mr. W., whose first one took five weeks.' Such stories do nothing but harm, and serve only to shatter that calm relaxation which is essential to a successful deliv . . . . to a successful Spring-cleaning.

I shall attempt in this article to answer a few of the questions most commonly put to me about Spring-cleaning. But before this, it is essential for husbands to have the right attitude in general. Discuss it with your wife, and try to see that Spring-cleaning is not simply the result of a blind pleasure-urge on her part. Above all, do not resent it. You are partners in a great enterprise that has gone on since the beginning of time. Without Spring-cleaning, the race would die out. In the days of cave-women, it was only when the year's collection of stones and bones was moved out that there was room for more food, for more life, more progress. Today, in this great act of bringing a brand-new home into the world, you are carrying on the torch for posterity, ensuring that your country is not buried under piles of old newspapers, choked with dust, or dead from boredom through looking at furniture in the same position for two or even three years. You should have a real love and sense of wonder for this vast potential power in your wife, who fertilises you and your home, and enables you to shed a skin, like a snake. Even if you have a hard time (and even today it is no good denying that modern knowledge is sometimes powerless to avoid complications, such as heavy paint bills, or long uncomfortable periods when all the chairs are upside-down in between the main upheavals) try to relax; think of that magic moment when, for the first time, you will see your wonderful new home.

A word to wives. Be forbearing with your husband at this time. If he has strange cravings, for unusual drinks perhaps, or if he flies into unreasonable passions, humour him. Remember that this is nature's way of showing that his time is near; he is about to produce wonderful new paints, new distempers and samples for curtains and carpets from his pocket. So give him the stability and rest that he so deeply needs from you now.

In a long experience of such cases I have found that those on the threshold of an ' event ' usually have more or less the same queries. Here are some of the main ones.

Should I have my Spring-cleaning at home or in hospital?

This is always a difficult question to answer. Ideally speaking, the unique bond between husband and wife at this time demands that you should have it naturally in your own home. Unfortunately, however, modern civilised man is not like the sturdy people of peasant countries, where the breadwinner often carries on in the fields within a matter of hours after his hovel has been swept out. Modern mental hospitals, with every resource at their disposal for dealing with badly frayed nerves in emergency cases, are a facility one cannot afford to overlook. And today there is also a growing tendency for men to have their Spring-cleaning in residential clubs or hotels. Generally speaking, this decision is largely determined by economics; if you live in a small house you will probably find it more convenient to stay there.

Is it dangerous to have one every year?

No. Provided proper care is taken there is no reason why a healthy man should not go on having Spring-cleanings right up to his seventieth year.

We have been married for seven years but have not had a Spring-cleaning yet. The doctor says I am quite normal. What should I do?

First satisfy yourself, honestly, that you have no hidden fears or reservations. Then you should have a frank talk with a reputable firm of interior decorators. But there is no way of telling whether the fault lies with your wife until *after a successful Spring-cleaning by them*, and this is why it is vitally necessary to be honest with yourself first. Artificial methods of this kind, unless used with the help of contractors who have been personally recommended to you, can be fraught with danger. Many men who have mistakenly used them, thinking unjustifiably that the fault lay with their wives, have suffered for years after the event from after-effects such as ' Inverted Pocket ' ' Bill Shock ' and ' Wasp's Disease ' (in which the victim cries out incessantly that he has been stung).

What diet do you recommend?

As a general rule I always advise, as part of the layette, a large number of tins . . . in the average household, about forty. But I have known many successful cases, of average duration (seven to ten days) where the patient has managed entirely on sandwiches. These, however, are rather rich in carbo-hydrates, and in any case the effort of opening tins is quite enough for the average patient, who should conserve as much energy as possible for the task in hand. The tins should, however, be varied by one or two very large meals, at which the wife may or may not be present, in a hotel. The main thing to remember is plenty to drink.

Ought I to help by moving smaller articles of furniture, filling buckets, etc?

On no account. Nature has fore-ordained an active rôle for women, a passive one for men. Women are physically equipped to find food and nourishment for their partners while they are going through this phase. Your job is to produce, after the quiet of a calm gestation, the spiritual and financial resources for the grand mutual task of transformation of the house. This is quite enough. Leave the physical side of it to the woman, and relax. During your Spring-cleaning many delicate psychological factors come into play; and it is quite possible that you may feel a groundless ' guilt ' at the loving trouble which is being expended on you. You should ignore it; and a wise wife will help you to laugh these fears away.

BELLS AND BUTTONS

Most people are afraid of waiters and hotel-keepers. Who has not gone into a restaurant at an hour that, outside in the friendly street, seemed reasonable enough, but somehow becomes a gross breach of some unwritten law once you are inside? Chairs are placed upside-down on tables, and salt cellars are collected, and gipsy musicians put on their black overcoats; and a row of silent waiters, as secret as the Etruscans, stand at the back of the room as though they had just come from, or were just going to, a meeting concerned with some obscure and rather sinister interest nothing whatever to do with their trade of refreshment and shelter.

The eyes of hotel people do not look at you and say Thou. The uncertain youngish men in hotel offices and *caisses* look up at you, from conversations in another language over large account books; and no matter what country, what pavement is on the other side of the revolving door, you feel more human kinship with the casual passers-by than you do with these hotel people.

It is, however, only when you are abroad in non-Nordic countries that you realise what is behind that veiled expression in their eyes. It is not so much hostility as withdrawal and bafflement. And what they are baffled at, these Latin hotel-keepers, is the Victorian English conception of cleanliness and godliness so arbitrarily imposed on their carefree, vinous world. There are two things that will always baffle them – baths and electricity.

I came across a superb example of this in Cyprus recently. Let no one imagine that there are not good hotels in Cyprus. On the contrary, they are extremely well organised, listed into five classes by the Government, and to get even into the fifth class they have to have a bath and running water. I would like to live for ever in Cyprus, preferably at Famagusta. Well, I had the good fortune to accompany the Inspector of Hotels, a charming Cypriot, when he examined a hotel of this fifth class, in an idyllic little town up in the hills. It was a clean, whitewashed place, and we were conducted up an outside staircase to a large, bare room with a stone floor. It was entirely empty but for a brand new, streamlined bath and a mirror. No pipes and no water. The bath just looked big and silly, like a stranded whale.

I do not understand modern Greek. But the drift of the animated conversation, which more and more people came up from the courtyard to watch, was quite clear to me. The proprietor was obviously saying: ' There you are, I've got your damn bath. *Now* can I be registered?' as though a bath were a kind of magic talisman, something the

Government required to be adored, like the statue of the Emperor in early Christian times. And my friend was pointing out gently that a bath was no use without water.

I caught the word ' radio,' and the Inspector told me afterwards that he was making the powerful point that you might as well have a radio without electricity. At this the proprietor shifted his ground and said that the peasants who used his hotel didn't want baths – not in a *hotel*, anyway.

Other hotel people, outside what one may call the Swiss orbit, take the view that if you *must* have water you might as well get some aesthetic pleasure from the business. I was once in an Italian hotel where the whole of one side of the bedroom was taken up by a vast carved affair like a baroque organ in some Bavarian church. Full of little fat boys, it was, and solid nymphs, and groaning, bearded men with lion's paws. I should not have been surprised if a hidden lever had caused tinkling fountains to issue from some of the hundreds of mouths, while languorous music played. But the centre portion simply hinged outwards, and there was a perfectly ordinary jug and basin.

As for electricity, hotel people regard this with the utmost distrust. They attempt to control it. The French, whose hotels are a cross between beehives and the Pyramids, with windowless corridors, and rooms entirely surrounded by other rooms, have automatic lights that snap off just when you have reached the worst part of the maze.

At my hotel in Athens the bedroom was full of extraordinary switches and buttons and bell-ropes; but the only switch for the bed-lamp was by the door. I could not find any switch for the bathroom, so I left the connecting door open for my bath, which I took in a curious thing like a porcelain armchair. It was impossible to submerge, so I pulled the cord for the shower. But this didn't operate the shower. It summoned a chamber-maid, who promptly knocked on the outside door. I shouted my apologies to her and she went away.

After I was dressed it occurred to me that my shoes could do with cleaning. I pressed a likely-looking and hitherto unnoticed button, and the bathroom was immediately flooded with light. I was quite surprised, in this hotel, when water, and not music or hot air, came through the washbasin taps.

I noticed that here they all looked at me in an even odder way than usual. Perhaps they were thinking: ' There goes that Englishman who is baffled by simple switches and electricity.'

LE SKI

The difference between aquatic art in England and in Mediterranean countries is the same as that between our literatures. There, the sea, or maybe the lake, is a placid blue surface on which classical skills may be demonstrated. Here, for many British children their first view of the sea, as they come round the last railway bend or breast the last garage-topped hill, is of a bumpy green field with tossing white flowers; when *we* swim in the sea we battle with it, we master it; we are empirical, romantic, we have to do with it; it is a creature, roaring or powerfully silent, with which we must cope at as many levels as Shakespeare did reality. But water like the lake of Geneva is simply an unquestioned background for the abstractions of virtuoso diving, of sailing, of classical crawl stroke – and, most of all, of water ski-ing.

When I joined the small queue by the jetty at the **end of** the *plage*, where it said simply S K I, the speed-boat was just coming in, towing a bronzed Swiss girl. She skimmed across the wake, glided to a stop in two feet of water, and waded competently out.

Next in the queue was an Irishman who had burnt himself in the sun to a degree that would have had me moaning in hospital; and his approach to water ski-ing showed a similar cheerful, amateur disregard for the advice of old hands. The tow-line suddenly jerked him off the jetty and dragged him off crouching, his arms outstretched. Perhaps, I thought, he did not know what the man shouting from the boat meant by ' *Faites plier les bras.*' He made one or two staggering attempts to get upright on his skis, and finally managed a half-standing position, in which he was towed a quarter of a mile, when the boat made a gentle turn and he went straight on and toppled over.

Somehow or other he was taken in tow again, and when he got back to the jetty there was a round of applause. Doubtless, I thought indulgently, for his tenacity.

It was only when I was fixing the skis that I had my own first doubts. They seemed to be about ten feet long; and the advice to press with the heels seemed difficult when I looked at the enormous length and weight of wood behind them.

The man in the motor-boat, circling gently round, threw me the towline, with a bar at the end, as I sat on the edge of the jetty with the skis in the water. It fell short, and in grabbing for it I fell in. The skis promptly floated upwards, so that I had to tread water with my hands only, and even that didn't keep my head above water all the time.

The Irishman helped me back on to the jetty. The man in the boat, who had shark-skin shorts and dark glasses, said: ' *Vous savez nager?*'

' *Oui. Je suis tombé seulement parce que vous n'avez pas jeté cette chose assez loin.*'

' Keep your arms bent and lean back,' said the Irishman, ' it's only a trick. It's all right once you get off.'

The boat moved out, the rope tautened, and suddenly there was an appalling jerk. One moment I was sitting on the jetty, the next I was being dragged along underneath roaring green water. It flashed through my mind that all this swimming is just a deception. Water is against us, really. I felt like Prometheus, or some completely lonely representative of the human will in a hostile chaos, as I pulled with every ounce of strength to stand up.

For a brief moment I saw the blurred shore, the two monstrous planks in front of me, the shark-skin man yelling incomprehensible French. I've done it, I thought, I've got off. Then I overbalanced forwards. The skis were dragged off, and I was pulled against a solid wall of water which stopped me from breathing until it occurred to me to let go the bar. I did.

I had imagined that we were by now in the middle of the lake; but as I turned to swim back I saw we had only come a hundred yards. I took a long time to get back, as the skis, which wouldn't float enough to support me, had to be pushed alternatively. There was no applause at the jetty.

' *Un autre essai*?' said the shark-skin man. ' *Oui*,' I said, hoping the pain in my ankle wasn't a sprain. ' *Je crois que j'ai un corps different de celui de cet Irlandais, car j'ai fait les mêmes choses. Pourquoi donc n'ai-je pas réussi*?' The shark-skin man shrugged.

One again the appalling jerk, the brief moment upright. This time I remembered to lean backwards. In fact I over-balanced backwards. The skis stayed on, and I had the same trouble keeping my head above water as when I fell in. The boat came round to me in a leisurely circle. ' *Vous voulez essayer d'ici?*' said the shark-skin man. ' *Oui,*' I gasped. He threw me the rope. It was even more difficult to stand up than after the ordinary start from the jetty. How that Irishman did it I shall never know.

Seven tries later, in the dying evening sun, they tried pulling me very slowly from another jetty, where it said ENFANTS. I got so that I could stay upright for about ten yards . . .

All the same, I'd like to see that shark-skin man swim to the end of Brighton Pier on a choppy day.

LE CAMPING

I can make people's cars go wrong just by sitting in them. I had further proof of this recently, when I went camping with my friend Harblow and his wife. We went in their Thing, an awful old blind-looking Morris Commercial which once rushed about London for five years delivering a national daily, after which Harblow bought it for £75. The Thing somehow manages to be both high and squat at the same time. People in saloon cars look uneasily all over its blank sides for the name of a firm, and are suddenly embarrassed to see Harblow, silk-scarved, beaming at them from his high seat. Farmers are misled by the Thing into feelings of compassion, gamekeepers and lorry-drivers into feelings of camaraderie.

They do not know that inside there are luxurious beds and a variety of American tents for guests. When we go camping we take Chianti and chops and Jane Austen and green peppers and madrigals. We pick twelve pounds of mushrooms, and are sorry for people in London.

Until they asked me they had never had any trouble with the Thing, and it didn't show its hand until we got to Essex, except for jumping out of gear now and again, and the spare wheel falling off. But as we turned off the road and bumped up a sodden green lane in a misty, private valley, among the tussocky fields and tasteless, pulpy old blackberries, I began, as always, to be afraid of Essex, afraid that the Thing would never get us back to London. I am never misled by the comfortable little weather-boarded old towns, or the ugly storage tanks of new Dagenham, into trusting Essex. It is a lonely county, lonelier than the Fells, because it is so near to London.

Even on ships, moving slowly down the muddy Thames from the bright heart of London out to the business of the seas and the clanking foreign ports, there is a moment of doubt, an intimation of death, in these brooding, misty flats. It is like being in a temperate-zone Suez Canal, with silent marshes and empty low fields instead of desert to make the careful navigation seem unreal. On land this feeling is much stronger. Essex is waiting to take over London. It wants to revert from agriculture, back to those tree-lined creeks that were illustrated by models in ' Land of Britain ' at the South Bank. I am sure those purple flowers on London bomb sites were sown by birds from Essex. It broods, dark, damp and lonely in the night. It waits.

We shook this feeling off, round our magic human fire, with the Chianti. Other people shook it off for us very early the next morning. That field, in the middle of nowhere, was alive with people. It was only just light when I was woken by the sound of male conversation. It was

Harblow, fully dressed, giving cigarettes to a man with a gun and a dog. Three silent women were purposefully gathering mushrooms. We decided to start the Thing and move on.

The self-starter made one low noise like a man grunting in his sleep, then was silent. We had to lift the bonnet to see where to fit the handle. Inside, the square engine looked severe and classical, like a gloomy little temple. Apart from the absurdly small carburettor, there were none of the out-houses that a modern engine has. We either had to wind from outside the enormous bumper, so that we were bent double, or stand inside and bang the handle against our knees. The compression was appalling. It was like turning a Marine Doxford engine. And when we did manage to turn, it only made a sucking noise and an evil yellow liquid squirted from the carburettor.

I tried to give it a continuous turn instead of one hopeful jerk. I got the handle round two and half times, then I tottered away, the landscape reeling. I asked Harblow if there was blood coming from my ears. An hour later, when Harblow and I were leaning panting against the radiator, the man with the gun came back. ' Ar,' he said, ' plug leads wet.' I said that didn't matter, water conducted electricity. It was my last attempt at urban superiority. He produced a comprehensive tool from his pocket and removed the plugs, drying them and the leads. He also removed, without comment, the hurricane lamp which Harblow had put there ' to warm the engine.' Then he went to the front and seized the handle. Harblow and I looked at each other surreptitiously. He was not a big man.

But he was wiry. He turned that monstrous engine round about twenty times, as easily as if it had been a sewing machine. There were signs of life. The man stepped back, not even red in the face. Harblow felt bound to emulate. He tried a continuous turn. It backfired and banged his knee. The man tried again, and the engine roared into life. I stamped vengefully on the accelerator. It cut out. Then the man started it *with the self-starter* . . .

On the way back, in the evening, the spare wheel fell off again. Later, the Thing stopped dead in the Mile End Road. Willing hands pushed us to a garage. After some investigation an attendant, cross at being called from a busy petrol queue, informed us, with a strange look, that the positive lead had jumped off the battery. The dynamo had fused the side and rear lights . . .

They haven't asked me again.

MISS!

One of the best examples of man's tendency to hold on to an ideal long after experience has rudely shattered it may be seen in our attitude to the theatre bar in the interval. When we are working, in the practical daytime, and the anticipation of a night at the theatre flits into our minds, we see ourselves like people in an advertisement, in some elegant foyer with palms and flowers and flunkeys; men are clean-cut, in elegant clothes, with that standard, young-lieutenant-colonel kind of face; one hand in trousers pocket, the other holding a cigarette. Girls are in ballet-length dresses, smiling up at escorts. In some way we too are actors, living in a world rather brighter and larger than our own.

If we are among those who have refreshment in the interval this is a much more formal, crisp and studied act than having it anywhere else. In this mental picture we have, there seem to to be about twenty-five minutes for relaxed, elegant talk about the play. No rude bells sound in this dream, no one ever has just beer, or coffee. And, most of all, there is no hint of the sordid struggle by which drinks are actually obtained in real life. The mind closes over this aspect of it like a self-sealing petrol tank.

Now I come to think of it, though, nobody else does seem to have this struggle except me, because all the other people in the bar are terrific personalities. It is only I who seem to be a normal, humdrum man, unable to attract the servers.

Every time I try to get a drink in a theatre bar I make a resolution to come next time on stilts, making myself nine feet high, to wear a red beard, and to demand drink with Latvian oaths. I stand sideways-on to the bar, and gradually work forward until I have one elbow on it, and finally two. But before I can do this the man in front, holding two glasses, steps back from the counter. I politely make way for him, and somebody on the other side of him immediately steps into his place. I adopt a kind of twin personality, turning round with a gay smile to the girl who is waiting for me, just to show her I am not having a round with some boon companion I have discovered in the press, and then return very unsmilingly indeed to the struggle.

When I do get to the front, I am always either faced by a large bowl of flowers or I am at the bend in the bar, or in a kind of no man's land between two servers who, if they ever hear the first two syllables of my despairing cry, ' Two light – ,' hiss ' Just a minute ' crossly at me through teeth which are holding a pound note. Normally they don't say anything at all; they are too busy flying up and down whisking bottles open for people who seem to be ordering enough refreshment for a Watteau country picnic.

H

Yet the other people have such personality that they can get served simply by speaking in cool, authoritative voices from wherever they happen to be. 'Six champagnes, please,' says a plummy-voiced, well-bathed man in a bird's-eye suit, who is standing *behind* me. I have a strange feeling that I am getting smaller and smaller.

Sometimes, when I get a seat at the end of a row, the moment the curtain has come down on the first act I rush to what is often called the saloon (this is one of those words that are often printed but never spoken, like Passengers Alighting, and Aerated Table Waters, and Luncheon). Often it is on the other side of the theatre, so that after I have run up and down stone steps so long and untheatrical that I am surprised not to find myself coming out under Blackfriars Bridge, the place is full when I get there. But if it is on my side, there often happens something very eerie indeed. *Nobody else comes.*

There is the bar all right, with brown linoleum and a little geyser affair with low blue flames, making burnt-smelling coffee. There is a shelf with three or four bottles on it. And there is a woman in black, like a *concierge*. But, as I say, nobody comes.

I have an urge to shout, or sing, for I have a lurking fear that my reflection will walk out of the glass at me, or that an eighteenth-century flower-seller will come in, or that the woman in black will suddenly point at me with a horrible wheezing laugh. I begin to have the same feelings about the theatre that Muslims have about artists – that God will look at the paintings they have done and then say: ' All right, now make them talk.'

I drink my beer and wish I had waited in a queue for it; even if the queue is full of pushers, at least they are human beings.

STOVE IN

Reading the articles on ' Rethinking our Future ' in the
Observer recently, I had a feeling analogous to that on
reading the lives of saints. There, in an intellectually
convincing scheme, is an ideal of heroic virtue. There are
many excellences in it that one could emulate – and then
comes this one thing, the very thought of which makes
one's mediocre soul shrink: facing torture, or kissing leper's
sores.

On a lower plane, it is the same with Our Future. At a
pinch I could face most of the things recommended. I
could do without American films. I could, indeed do, work
on Saturday mornings. I am reconciled intellectually to
the adventure of turning motor-car production over to jet
airliners. But when it comes to fuel economy I am simply

not big enough to give up the ' wasteful domestic fire.'

This is not only because of its visual fascination – for flames have the same hypnotic combination of rest and motion as the sea – but also because I am beset with doubts whether, if I *did* make the supreme gesture for the pound sterling and get one of those dreary closed stoves, the nation and I would be much better off anyway. Not if it was like my friend Harblow's stove.

Not that Harblow got it for patriotic reasons (some other thing – giving up private motoring, perhaps – would be the impossible gesture for him). He was mad about it. From the moment he read the pamphlet about warming the whole house for two months with three hundredweights of coal, he was starry-eyed. Alas, it didn't work. Or if it did, it was only at the cost of labours which would make me quite unfit for any other occupation.

I have never seen anything so *obstinate* as that stove. It was a silly little round thing, sitting on a bed of concrete that Harblow had installed at enormous expense in his basement kitchen. It grinned at you. The first thing Harblow found out about it was that it would use only that artificial fuel which looks like pickled walnuts. Harblow had two manholes over his cellar, and every time the coalman came there were frantic, detailed instructions to drop these *ovoids*, I think they were called, through the second manhole; not through the first, where the proper coal for my fire (I had a flat in his house) was kept. And always the coalman would drop the ovoids on the coal. Then we would have to take a hurricane lantern into the cellar and separate the stuff into two heaps. The only way to do it accurately enough was by hand. If you put one lump of ordinary coal on the stove it would go out.

To light the thing you had to follow a ritual as precise

and intricate as the ordering of an Egyptian king's tomb. When it was finally going it would never do any of the secondary jobs that you expect from a fire. You could never light a cigarette from it. If you put a spill in, it just smouldered until your hand got too hot to hold it. It was supposed to burn rubbish, too. But there was only an absurd little lid at the top, and if you put some small rubbish through here it just lay on top of these cold ovoids and put out what fire there was lower down.

If, on the rare occasions when the top ovoids were burning, you put a kettle on the lid, it was one hour fifteen minutes before it even began to sing, let alone boil. Nevertheless, the lid was always too hot to remove by hand. There was a special gripping tool for it, which for some reason was always getting lost, buried under the ovoids in the cellar.

The only time it ever went really well was in the middle of the night. Every now and then the household would be wakened by a curious *whizzing* noise, punctuated by *jub-a-jub*, *JUNK*, *ajunka-JUNK*. Doors would be opened. Lights would go on in the bathroom, Harblow would turn on the hot tap, which let out nothing but steam for some time; the entire system was boiling. Then he would have to run off three baths full of scalding water.

On other nights it would go out, and other sounds would be heard – Harblow shovelling, dropping the hot lid, falling over his ovoid scoop and cursing down in the cellar. The odd thing was that he never lost faith in it; he was convinced that there was some little thing he had forgotten, and once he found what it was the stove would justify its maker's wild claims.

That thing ruled his life. When he and his wife went out at night, nine-tenths of their instructions to the baby-sitter were about baffles and dampers and ovoids, not about the baby. And quite right, too. There is nothing that stove would have liked better than to burn the house down, baby and all, the moment his back was turned.

Of course, it probably *did* save fuel. But unless one is a Harblow or a hero, it hardly seems worth while.

PROBLEM PIPES

I wish now I had never told Harblow about my burst pipes. He has never ceased to be superior about my disastous attempts at a Wiped Joint when we were both on a course in the Signals. There were only enough bits of cable for four joints, and the corporal instructor used Harblow's to demonstrate. I amazed the corporal by using two whole sticks of solder. All I seemed to be able to do was to build a huge pyramidical mound of solder on the upper side. Although I wiped long and furiously, until smoke began to come from the wiping pad, I simply could not get it to stick underneath. Any further applications of solder ran off this great stalagmite and formed a rather lovely filigree silver disc on the floor.

I had, therefore, accepted the fact that I can no more plumb, than I can butch, carpent, or farry. But when, during the cold spell, the bath began to fill mysteriously with dirty water *from the plughole upwards* I felt I had to investigate. I did so with some trepidation, because house plumbing has always seemed to me to be one of those things which, with a little accidental readjustment, might be made into something catastrophically *else*. Just joining a few wrong ends of those loops and whorls of piping going all round the house might, perhaps, turn the whole system into a sort of gigantic French horn, with the bath as the bowl of the horn; a vacuum caused by the emptying of the tank might then cause air to rush through the pipes, blowing a terrible deep sombre blast on the bath which would make the whole place fall down, like the walls of Jericho.

Even plumbing should obey the law of gravity; but I found that the outlet from the bath split into two branches, of which one, it is true, did go down to the ground. The other went *up*, to the tank in the roof. A man likes to know the reason for these things, even if the nearest he can get to a real plumber is a man like Harblow.

When I first telephoned him he tried to brush it off by saying knowledgeably ' Ah, the one that goes up is a *vent* pipe.' I pointed out that unless it was to vent the bath water in a kind of spray over the roof a vent pipe was for air, not water, whereas this one indubitably went into the tank. So he came round. We took hurricane lamps, pemmican and reindeer meat into the bathroom, and together we made this plan. ' Time spent in recce.,' said Harblow , ' is seldom wasted.'

' It is clear,' he said, ' that pipes C and D are frozen, and that is why your bath keeps filling with water through the problem pipe.' He said this with the air of one announcing a new planet to the Royal Society.

'Surely,' I said, 'if that were true there would be a continual circulation of water up A, through the tank, through the problem pipe and back to earth through C and D without ever going into the bath at all.'

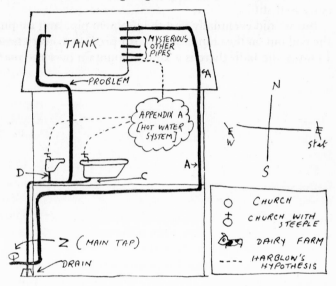

But Harblow is a man who refuses to be permanently mystified. In the end he returned obstinately to his first theory, about the vent pipe, with modifications. 'It was originally a vent pipe in the plan.' he said, 'but when the man was installing the tank in 1844 he found the loose ends of the Mysterious Other Pipes, and not being very good at reading plans, he assumed they all went into the tank. All we have to do therefore, is to find which is the end of the problem pipe and detach it.'

Harblow got out his kit, which included one of those roaring burners. We had omitted to turn off Z, and of course the first pipe he melted away turned out to be A. I put my foot through the ceiling in recoiling from the terrible gout of water from A. It trickled through the house while we rushed downstairs to turn off Z, which was very rusty and stiff.

But we did eventually find the problem pipe and we put the end out on the chimney. Just as I predicted, every time I empty the bath there is a kind of fountain over the roof.

DOWN AMONG THE Z-MEN

As the convoy, of which I was amazingly in charge, trundled through the old villages, in the solemn adult game that the Army loves to call a ' scheme,' there was in the high hum of the truck wheels a ghostly sense of the past. Although it is undoubtedly hard work, there is something curiously dream-like about service in the Z Reserve. It is like the dream in which one is back at school; one has got one's Higher Certificate, all one's friends have left, yet here one is, among all these boys, feeling a vague embarrassment. Although we ourselves had no dealings with the National Servicemen, one was constantly aware of them, boys with blank, unformed faces, who wore civilian clothes in the evening.

The nineteenth-century homogeneity of the Army (I remembered the poignant ' Lights Out ' on the autumn air at Winchester in 1939) seemed to have given way to this Nato feeling – a process which began some time in 1943, when even the military alphabet was Americanised, and Ack Beer, as British as plum and apple, became the curiously florid Able Baker. (Who is this Baker? What does he *want?*)

There was also the additional unreality of being an officer. It seemed surrealist that I should be in charge of these admirable, loyal Z-men, covered with campaign ribbons, when my last command had been a section of neurotic Bengali linemen. They had mutinied in the Indian Artillery, so the Army had masterfully transferred them *en bloc* into the Signals. They all had the School Certificate, and were forever attempting suicide.

Leading this Z convoy, I was worried principally about two things. One was every officer's nightmare – that I should lead these vast trucks and trailers into a cul-de-sac on a narrow road. I believe this happens to everybody once. It had happened to me once in India. All the sign-posts were in Malayalam. We had gone through a town, and after about thirty miles of desolation I noticed that we were going into the setting sun, whereas we should have been going north. Mountains had begun to close in on the road.

I halted the convoy and looked wisely at the map. Presently a solitary truck appeared in a cloud of dust from the other direction. It contained a Captain in the R I A S C, who said I was lucky to see him. He was on a monthly tour, and this road simply petered out in the mountains. I thanked him, and hastily turned the convoy round. I was rather surprised that he did not disappear in a clap of thunder. This time, in domestic East Anglia, with these Z-men, I knew I could expect no such preternatural help . . .

But I found the map-reference all right; and once the camp was established, the cook was cooking, and our huge wireless set happily sending out messages about Blueland and Redland, I began to think of my second worry – my camp kit. For in one of those gestures which are at the same time touching and slightly mad, the Army had issued to each Z-officer one of those colossally heavy bundles which contain the equivalent of the furniture of a small house, only all in canvas. There is a canvas bed, a canvas bucket, indeed a canvas bath; one would not be surprised, as one delves in this bottomless bag, to find a canvas chest-of-drawers.

There is even a canvas chair, all wooden legs and metal rods and straps, which is supposed to come out like the ones film directors use, with their names on; the kind of chair which one imagines being offered to the Chilean Military Attaché, with polished riding boots, at some Salisbury Plain manoeuvres in 1929. I could make it up only with the back bent forward over the seat, and even then it collapsed when I sat on it.

The fact is, I was embarrassed by this luxury. The Z-men had two large tents, and groundsheets, and they had magically produced a lot of straw from somewhere. It looked more comfortable than any camp bed *I* have ever known. Nevertheless, I thought, in the loneliness of power, I had better sleep in a truck. I assembled my bed after dark in the only available one – the ration truck, which was just wide enough for the bed, but not for me to get round it and make it properly. As there were only two hurricane lamps in the entire camp, I had to work in the dark.

The truck was parked on a slope and unidentified tins kept rolling underfoot. When I knelt on one end of the bed the other end jumped up, bringing down more tins. I was

uneasily aware that somewhere in the truck there was
something sticky. I struck endless matches but could only
see these tins. Three times I went out and washed my
hands, but the stickiness came back. Eventually the bed
was made.

I turned in at 1.30 a.m. Rain came through the end-
flaps. At 2.30 a.m. I woke, hideously cramped and cold.
There was a misty silence – the roaring generator which
supplied our wireless set had suddenly stopped. I got up to
investigate, in the rain, and then I made an appalling
discovery. My *ears* were sticky. There was jam all over the
pillow.

THEATRE OPERATION

When I found that the amateur dramatic society which I had joined always gave one performance at a hospital, it was too late to withdraw. I ought to have withdrawn earlier, anyhow; the friend who ran it had told me they were going to do *You Can't Take It With You*, and I had hoped to be cast as the delightful lunatic who makes fireworks in the basement and ends Act One with an enormous explosion. I hadn't bargained for playing Captain Wickham, in *Pride and Prejudice*, to a helpless audience of convalescents.

The hospital was in North London, in what had once been a country estate where landaulettes rolled up to a lawn dotted with parasols; but now, as we arrived with the fruits of our winter rehearsal, it was just a sad urban wood surrounded by villas. The place was deathly silent. The company, carrying suitcases, assembled in the Gothic porch, under a Victorian coat-of-arms, and instinctively stopped chattering when the producer pulled a great wrought-iron handle, and a distant bell was heard.

I was suddenly filled with panic. Although we had been assured that ' our friends at the hospital ' were looking forward to our visit, it seemed to me now an appalling presumption that we should attempt to create the warm magic of the theatre in this naked, functional place. Wildly I tried to recall what I had been told about Noel Coward, alone on a bare platform in the Middle East, gradually getting five thousand restive troops to eat out of his hand . . . after all, we should at least have bed screens for curtains.

The men changed in a room full of white, glass-fronted cabinets containing little bottles. There was the awful coconut smell of make-up. We were all given a little duplicated slip which said ' *There is no back cloth.* If you come off R and have to reappear L, go up hall steps, along passage, through little door on right, down iron staircase, through door, through recreation room, up stairs. Vice versa for L to R.'

I should have liked very much to practise this route before going on, since it looked as deceptively detailed as the instructions, shouted from other people's sitting-rooms when you are in their kitchen, about how to find the sugar. They always have to come themselves in the end, just as I should have liked the writer of these directions to demonstrate his route. But there was no time. Our Mozart divertimento stole out across the darkened Victorian drawing-room. The gracious, complicated sentences began. ' *It is a reflection on every gentlemen present that one so fair should lack an escort . . .* ' and suddenly I was offstage, R.

My splendid officer's uniform had no pockets, so I had

lost the directions. There was nobody to ask. I went up the hall steps. Along passage. Little door – no, not that one. Another door – good, here's the iron staircase. An outside fire-escape. It was raining. I got half-way down, then I met Lady Catherine de Burgh, in a billowing yellow dress, coming up. My sword stuck in the railings. I got out of the belt and backed up the stairs to let her pass. As she brushed by the sword belt she freed it. It fell with a clatter on to some dustbins below. A nurse opened a window, and betrayed no surprise when a British officer of the Napo-leonic War period on the fire-escape asked her for a box of matches. I went right down to the bottom, and began striking matches to find my sword among the dustbins, in the pouring rain.

I opened a door, but it revealed the boiler-room. I asked an astonished man with a shovel where the recreation room was. ' Next floor,' he said. I felt glad it wasn't a mental hospital. On the next floor there were two doors, one locked. The unlocked one opened into a long kitchen, full of maids at aluminium-topped tables. I strode down this room, with my sword; there was no time for dallying, my big scene with Lydia must be nearly due, and there was a big, important sort of door at the other end which looked as if it led into some more public domain. I was half-way down before I saw it was only a cupboard.

I strode back again, and up the iron staircase. I arrived, breathless and wet, on the same side of the stage that I had come off, just in time for my scene with Lydia, who was looking expectantly for me in the other direction. I am sure the patients, or rather the audience, thought I was going to pant out the news of Waterloo rather than make love.

I discovered two more doors into that kitchen; in fact

I went through it four times. They must have thought I was a stage army. After the play I got the first glimpse I have ever had behind medical inscrutability. We were invited to refreshments in the recreation room. When I saw the liberal bar and the enormous array of excellent food, I quite saw why it had been locked.

POLICEMAN'S PLEASURE

No part of the community has a more secret, indrawn life than the police. Perhaps it is because we are all aware of them, alone at night in the wet streets under creaking signs, preserving civilisation against the windy dark for us until to-morrow, that we all make this mistake of trying jolly, man-to-man talk with them. But they always withdraw into their huge secret, making us feel as though we had cut across some formal boundary, like arguing with the pulpit from the nave, or shouting advice to actors. They make us feel like Oscar Wilde – over-articulate, defiantly gay, but caught like a rat in a trap.

Only last week I experienced this, right outside the OBSERVER office. Tudor Street is one of a network of narrow lanes, where enormous lorries with rolls of paper come, like liners lost in a canal, and men in caps direct the flow of evening-paper vans. The trick in parking at the OBSERVER is to wait until one of these moves off and then nip in smartly. I had been doing this for months when, last week, a policeman said: ' How long are you going to stay here?'

' I don't know,' I said. ' I work here.' I hadn't meant it facetiously at all, but I regretted it immediately.

' You can't park here more than twenty minutes.'

I asked him what I was *supposed* to do. He said I must go to a car park, and when I asked him where the nearest one was he replied, without moving a muscle, ' Seacoal Lane.'

Where on earth was that, I wanted to ask. Did he really expect me to pick my way across the City to this Elizabethan wharf, where chaldrons were unloaded from what were doubtless called butty-boats? Was it simply the policeman's endless desire to keep us all Moving Along There, paralleled by an instruction to the buttymen at Seacoal Lane to take their lumbering wains to Tudor Street? Did it exist at all? Perhaps

> *Beside a public bar in Lower Thames Street*
> *The pleasant whining of a mandoline,*
> *And a clatter and a chatter from within*
> *Where fishmen lounge at noon: where the walls*
> *Of Magnus Martyr hold*
> *Inexplicable splendour of Ionian white and gold.*

Or was it a huge policeman's joke, a façade behind which we were all ultimately human friends, like the people in Chesterton's ' The Man Who Was Thursday?'

It is against this background of policemen's undoubted *otherness* that we must consider the news that a Sunbeam Talbot car driven by police officers is entered in the Monte Carlo Rally. At first sight it might seem extraordinary; but on closer examination it is all of a piece with this ambiguity of policemen. For it is impossible to guess whether they are going as people, or officially.

Perhaps the former is the case. Perhaps they long for non-functional motoring, but know they can never do anything gay in those solemn Humbers they have, with searchlights and gongs, as long as they stay in England.

Perhaps their intention is to flash through the Alps, negotiating the stumbling-blocks with a contemptuous skill learnt long ago at Hendon Police College, and they are really bent on winning the final *Concours de Confort*. Beautiful policewomen in clouds of chiffon will sit beside them as they glide, flower-bedecked, under the rococo balconies in the Mediterranean sunshine, to cheers and admiring murmurs of ' *Ah, les jolies flic-girls!*' And at night in the Casino, there will be gay but discreet gambling, well within the £25 limit.

Or is there more to it? Perhaps, as they roar down the main street in some little town in the Haute-Savoie, a gendarme will make a sign to them. Scattering the crowds lining the route, they will screech round the corner into a side road, leap out and surround a house. They thunder on the door. A tousled blonde appears. ' *Madame*,' says one of them carefully, ' *nous cherchons un certain M. Bodgershall.*' She pales. ' Cor!' she shrieks, ' the perishin' cops, *Alf!*' They brush past her, kick open a door. ' Alfred Cleghorn Bodgershall, I have a warrant for your extra-dition . . . . . '

Or perhaps, unworthy thought, they will ask British sightseers at Monte Carlo to show their currency forms. We do not know. With the police, we shall *never* know.

WALGING AGAIN

Some time ago I wrote about a newspaper report that
' police in King's Cross saw fifty to seventy youths walging
in Caledonian Road,' and I sympathised with the police in
their helplessness before this terrifying manifestation of the
twentieth-century herd man, ' this blind, horrible,
corporate movement, halfway between bulging and
waltzing, this mute, resistless pressure, welling outwards
from a half-formed lubberly totemic dance – there is no
precedent for walging.'

Well, there is a precedent now. It is true that we have
not seen many reports of walging, because there has been a
natural desire to hush up this awful phenomenon, the
modern equivalent of the dancing fever that swept Europe

after the Black Death. But recently there has been a quite open admission that it can no longer be repressed – that in fact it has the ultimate moral sanction, that of the BBC. Not long ago in the ' Manchester Guardian,' I read this:

> Four hundred scientists from industry, Government Departments and the universities yesterday watched a demonstration of nearly perfect colour television at the BBC's research station at Kingswood Warren, Surrey. A scene showing a man walging on the sun-lit roof in front of a gaily-coloured garden umbrella was reproduced on the television screen inside the laboratory . . .

Does it not freeze the blood, the thought of these 400 scientists calmly watching a *demonstration* of walging? We have come a long way from those policemen in King's Cross, striving with inherited peasant sanity to contain this communal neurosis. Alas for the police, alas for the peasants, alas for Europe! Far above them, cold-eyed intellectuals have been committing a new *trahison des clercs*, so successfully that now the inner temple, the BBC, has fallen.

Do you not see them, these 400 scientists, myopic pale-faced men in black suits, coming in closed cars past the trim Surrey gardens, blinking in the sunlight and putting on dark glasses as they get out at Kingswood Warren, which looks like an innocent roadhouse with those gaily-coloured umbrellas on its roof (for roadhouses *are* innocent, compared with walging)?

Ah, you peaceful Surrey bungalow dwellers, watering your roses, you little knew what hideous social breakdown was being coldly assisted in your midst that afternoon! For the BBC, which entertains millions who, paradoxically, are rarely in listening groups of more than four, has taken the fatal step in introducing walging to the British family unit.

Hitherto walging was at least a mass phenomenon still restricted to spontaneous outbreaks in large cities, as in the case of those fifty to seventy youths at King's Cross. We who are aware of walging only in this way, as a mass function, can scarcely imagine by what monstrous technique a single man can express his loss of identity in a *nonexistent* mob. Nor can we conceive what plans these scientists formed for the advancement of walging in industry, Government Departments, and the *universities*. We can, and do, note how these three fields are listed in order of their susceptibility to walging.

We begin with industry, the urbanised mass, the background against which walging has already appeared. It is easy enough to imagine industrial scientists insinuating walging into the works canteen dances, although difficult to imagine why, since once it gets out of hand and the foundries and drawing offices and annealing shops are distorted with the unholy motion, the very walls bulging as in a Disney cartoon, it is hard to see how the scientists can retain their managerial control.

So, too, with the Government Departments. It will be a simple matter for the scientists, Higher Executive Officers, working at bare tables in the converted bathrooms of vast, dirty mansion flats built in 1903, to put notices about walging among the hundred others fluttering on the notice board by the gilt-latticed lift that doesn't work. But what will they do when they want a notice typed, say, about import restrictions on hot process roll feed transfer blocking foil templates, and, going along to the typing pool, they hear the dread mindless ululations of walging from far down the corridor?

Most alarming of all is the fall of the ultimate intellectual citadels, the universities. In so far as walging can be related to any known categories of humanist civilisation, it is, in a horrible inverted way, nearer to art than science. What will happen when the great glubbering tidal wave comes seething into the quiet quadrangles, when the last sanctuary of the Western intellect is violated?

Is it really true that the scientists have thought of all this, that they were actuated by a cold death-wish? If that is so, we can put our trust only in the Arts Faculties and hope *they* at least will make a last, hopeless stand against it.

DOCTOR CALIGARI'S BALLOON

In a barber's shop I always have a slight feeling of guilt, or at least of unease, at having lived so long without properly exploring this curious world of theirs, where the business of life is suddenly stopped among the calm smell of unguents. What is a vibro-massage, and why do I not have the courage to find out? Why cannot I talk easily to the barber, like the man in the next chair?

He is always the same kind of man, with a ruddy face and an air of effortless but somehow dubious wealth. He is always fed by the barber with the right questions, such as: 'You been to America, sir?', and of course he has. He 'flew in last week,' in fact. Or he has 'just picked up a Jaguar.' Or he knows all about boxing.

I restrict my demand to a brusque 'Trim, please,' although secretly I long to try this vibro-massage, from which I am sure I should emerge equally ruddy, with

gong-like Holst chords humming in my clear, tingling head
– *vibrant*, in fact; but this man, still talking about Ezzard
Charles, has mysterious, effeminate-looking operations
that even involve the use of a *hairnet*.

Gloomily I reflect on the barber's shop as a weak social
survival of those great Roman baths where elegant and
relaxed conversation went on in clouds of steam. By the
time the barber gets to the razor bit round my ears I am
adrift in a lonely sea of ideas which would be impossibly
outré in conversation, compared with the Jaguar man's –
ideas like Petronius or Quintilian languidly asking
'*Aliquid habes pro tres triginta?*' ('Have you anything for the
three-thirty?') . . .

At my last haircut I decided to try the Wilfred Pickles
approach; I asked the barber if it was difficult to get
apprentices these days. The response was gratifying, for he
had just seen on his television set a film about the training
of barbers in Germany. It was not, however, the pity and
terror of this tragic subject that moved him.

Before I had mentally filled in the details – a mad Emil
Jannings in some terrible Expressionist shaving saloon,
with the walls closing in and corpses waiting on the
benches reading frayed copies of '*Simplicissimus*,' the
barber went on indignantly: 'It showed the trainees
shaving balloons, and they said it was a new idea. Why, I
did that when I was an apprentice twenty-five years ago.'

Shaving balloons! Even the old Ufa people couldn't
have thought up anything as macabre as that. I saw Emil
Jannings more clearly now, barking orders to the row of
young boys, grimly lathering balloons which, in a happy
non-capitalist society, they would have been childishly
chasing outside in the Tiergarten. '*Ein, zwei, drei*,' he
rasps. '*Beginnen sie die Ballonen zu rasen*,' and no sound is

heard but the squeaky noise of razor on rubber until a horrid pop; Jannings advances on the hapless apprentice, and is about to twist his ear when the doorbell tinkles and in comes a figure which sits down in the vacant chair.

Jannings approaches it obsequiously. A muffled, rubbery voice asks for a shave. Jannings now sees that the figure is merely an awful, stuffed simulacrum of a human body, but instead of a head it has a – no, it's too horible.

After all, I thought, this happened in our own England, twenty-five years ago. There would be a Cockney humour about it. ' *This perishin' balloon's going down.*' ' *That's the advanced course, mate – old man with wrinkles.*' I wondered how the apprentices got on with their first real faces, confronted with noses and lips after the simple curves of a balloon. Or was there, perhaps, a special barber's balloon, with proper features – with *hair*, even? And if so, whatever would it look like when deflated? What kind of expression would this balloon be made with?

One always thinks of balloons at fairs, having large moony smiles, floating with a balmy, withdrawn joy above the people earnestly seeking mechanical amusement. These balloons would require special faces, with the down-drawn mouth of all men when shaving.

Did they give the balloons vibro-massage too? And did some earnest but not very intelligent apprentice ever attempt a singe? Did the trainees ever get nightmares in which they nicked a man's chin and he *burst?* Above all, what of the man who first had this extraordinary idea? Do older barbers feel sorry for him, in his retirement, as he watches this inspiration taken up, like another British one, the tank, by more enterprising countries? . . .

But I couldn't ask any more questions – not with the Jaguar man there.

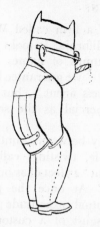

GILA MONSTERS

Zoology and the classification of animals are at once the most precise and the most doubtful of sciences; precise in the tradition of Linnaeus, doubtful in that when we actually go to the zoo and look into the animals' eyes we wonder uncomfortably if we know anything about them at all. As Martin Buber says: ' An animal's eyes have the power to speak a great language. Independently, without needing co-operation of sounds and gestures, most forcibly when they rely wholly on their glance, the eyes express the mystery in its natural prison, the anxiety of becoming . . . This language is the stammering of the first touch of spirit, before it yields to spirit's cosmic venture that we call man. But no speech will ever report what that stammering knows and can proclaim.'

These listening cows and sad monkeys, these ancient-dreaming elephants, these jerky-hopping, irrational-jumping birds, they can never be mere scientific subjects.

Still less can they be merchandise, and this is what gives

such poignancy to the catalogue of a firm called Wild Animals, Inc., of Silver Springs, California. It looks just like any other catalogue, with columns of names and figures and an order form on the back (' we guarantee live, healthy specimens delivered to express agent '), but the whole thing looks about as commercial as the ship's inventory of Noah's Ark.

Perhaps the most obvious disparity between counting-house arithmetic and the secret life, twisting, calling, strutting, of animals, occurs in the item ' 25 feet of assorted, large snakes (our selection) – $25.' At once the pro-liferation of nature makes contractual exactitude im-possible. We may imagine the disgust of a customer, expecting one magnificent snake 25 feet long, at receiving a seething box of 50 miserable 6 in. kraits.

In vain does the item ' skunks (demusked), $15 ea.' attempt to reassure us that the advertised product will fit into the average home as easily as a new lampshade. As we read of ' Humboldt's woolly monkeys', or of ' sooty-faced mangabeys', we become more and more aware that the naming of these creatures, far from putting them into a pigeon-hole and enabling us to forget about them, actually accentuates their otherness.

By a great effort of will it is possible to say ' my dog ' in the same way that one would say ' my boots ': but one could not say ' my sooty-faced mangabey ' without ex-panding on the theme, without entering into relationship. And it is significant that the most saturnine of all the animals, the reptiles, calling out to us from the slime, have the most pregnant and symbolic names of all. Southern Toads, for instance, at $3.00 per doz., are *bufo terrestris terrestris* which clearly means ' of the earth, earthy.' And what about Spadefoot Toads, *scaphiopus holbrookii holbrookii?*

What *nostalgie de la boue* led this Holbrookius into his swampy researches?

This is a document that could have appeared only in America, where no St. Patrick has yet driven out the snakes, where plumbing and drug stores have suddenly filled a continent that only recently belonged to animals; where business men go *hunting* at weekends. It is an attempt to build a bridge between the rational Græco-Roman libraries of Yale and Harvard and the strange, decadent life of the southern swamps – the South of writers like Truman Capote and Eudora Welty, in whose stories lonely people lie sweating in airless hotel rooms in small towns, beaten by the sterile northern cities, where reptiles are safely kept in zoos.

For there is no doubt that these classifiers have an unhealthy bias towards reptiles. What dreadful plan, by some wicked youth wishing to kill off the brother who stands between him and a vast estate, is foiled by the note: WE DO NOT SELL POISONOUS SNAKES TO MINORS WITHOUT PARENT'S CONSENT? On what errand is the express agent driving up the approach to this awful house in the marshes? He lugs a great packing case up the steps, mops his brow and rings the bell. A distant, rusty tintinnabulation is succeeded by a dank silence. Then there are shuffling footsteps over stone floors, a maniacal laugh from some high room, and the door is opened.

The express man blanches at the sight of the macabre family peering at him from the shadows, but he bravely stands his ground; swallowing, he sings 'Happy birthday to you,' and hands over the case. It contains a Gila Monster ($25 ea.). Behind him is his van. He has only to get in and press the self-starter to get back to the familiar road. He backs down the steps, but the monster . . . No, no!

THE LOSS FORCE

One of the mysterious ways in which the material world reminds us that we do not control it is by abstracting personal possessions from us. In our brash human way we then say that *we* have lost them; but in fact we have not done anything, we have been acted on by the Loss Force. This is analogous to, and much more mysterious than, Shaw's Life Force.

Who has not known that feeling, almost of terror, when one searches a room for a book that one saw five minutes ago? Yes, it was on that table, in the cosy, intellectually ordered world in which we were living before we missed it. But after this awful, this magical disappearance, we resort to methods of discovery which mere intellect tells us are mad.

We look under large articles of furniture that have not been moved for months. We telephone our friends and ask if they've borrowed it. We look in the bathroom, under the bed, more and more wildly. These are not rational acts; they are a kind of possessed ritual, to propitiate the Loss Force.

On a select band of us the Loss Force acts in a special manner, just as a kind of racial wisdom and innocence operates through the type of Dostoievsky's Idiot. People like me are dedicated to it. I lose pens and matches and glasses and handkerchieves all the time; and every four months or so there is a Grand Loss – a spare wheel, an overcoat, a typewriter (if that was only burglars, why didn't they take anything *else?*).

I have been able to organise my life on a rather beautiful, resigned acceptance of these facts. But it is a resignation that has only recently healed the scars made, three or four years ago, by the dreadful fear that I had been selected by the Loss Force *to lose other people's things as well.*

My friend Harblow, who had stayed on in the Army was, passing through London, and I put him up on a Friday night. He had business in South London on Saturday morning. I was working in Baker Street. We arranged to meet for lunch; and to save him carting his bag around I was to take it to the office and hand it over at the restaurant.

I got on the bus with his bag. Near Marble Arch I saw the bus I wanted for Baker Street coming down Park Lane. I leapt lightly off the first bus and on to the second. We had gone about 300 yards, to Portman Square, when I remembered Harblow's bag. For once this wasn't a crawler bus, but I got off it somehow. I hailed the first taxi that came—an incredibly old one, driven by a man like a walrus. Indeed, he seemed to be some sort of manifestation of the Loss Force. I could feel it in the air throughout that ghastly day, informing the cold grey buildings, making London hostile, brooding and unhelpful.

It seemed ludicrous to be chasing anything, even a bus, in this high, pram-like machine. Nevertheless, I breathlessly instructed the dotard to drive furiously down Wigmore Street, which is parallel to Oxford Street, and try to intercept the bus at Oxford Circus. We lumbered off. All the lights were against us. We got stuck in an appalling jam. No bus.

I telephoned London Transport and asked them what was the earliest hour at which a 12, a 17, or an 88 (for it could have been any of these) could be coming back again. They didn't seem at all taken aback by this appalling poser. I heard a rustle of pages, then a voice said, 11.31. So at 11.30 I stood outside the C and A. For two hours I stood at the head of the queue, looking in every bus, in the little place under the stairs, but never getting in. It must have looked mad. No bag.

I had a sad lunch with Harblow. The bag, he said, contained his service dress, his squash racket and clothes, his camera, pyjamas and shaving tackle, £15, all the papers for a court-martial in which he was the prosecuting officer on the following Monday. I saw the headlines, OFFICER GAVE FRIEND SECRET PAPERS, COURT TOLD. OFFICER HELD ON BUS BAG LOSS. MR. X TELLS COURT PSYCHIATRIST OF ' LOSS FORCE ' . . .

That afternoon I found out enough about London Transport's layout and running schedules to write the script for a training film. I made calls to countless garages. ' Just a minute,' a voice would say; and for a quarter of an hour I would hear hollow echoing bangs, and whistling, and engines, and cinema organ music; then the voice would say, ' No, I'm sorry ' . . . And all the time the crooks were photostatting the court-martial papers, sharing out the £15, taking the camera to a ' fence.' Or were they? Had the bag, in fact, just *disappeared?*

But at six o'clock the Loss Force realised it had got the wrong man. The bag was in a garage at Merton. Now if it had been *mine* . . .

BUCYRUS

One of the biggest errors made by the simple-minded townsman, as he jovially enters country pubs, imagining that the unseen villages behind the folded hills are just the same as this one, is his assumption that the countryside is catching up with *him*. He looks at the pylons and the wires on wooden poles, and smiles at the self-consciousness of rural electricity compared with his own, which comes smoothly underground. If he had eyes to see, he would realise that these pylons are just one more manifestation of a strange Force, half human and half a modern re-appearance of forgotten natural gods, that is *up to something* in the country.

Now, what is so enigmatic about all this is the attitude of the country people. Whose side are *they* on? The townsman, in their pubs, hearing them talk of the television, may think to recognise fellow souls. But is he right? Let him look again. Let him recall that initial feeling of interrupting a private joke between these scarf-headed women, dissolving into hoarse laughter at which he smiles uneasily, and these men in rubber boots. Where do they all go, disappearing off the main road in station waggons? How much do they know? Is there not something more than an uncomfortable feeling that they know how to deliver calves and he doesn't? Let him question the safe feeling that television makes us all one.

The more I travel in southern England, the more I am aware of extraordinary machines; big grey things, with hoppers and spindly arms. They are not simple combines. They have useless-looking wheels up in the air. Sometimes they are in fields, sometimes they are being towed purposefully, with that air of thinking quietly to themselves that snails have. They are taking up positions.

One night, one fateful night, something will be set in motion. The country air will be filled with clanking; these things will walk with a terrible tread over the fields, like awful iron insects. They will form rings round the ports. Motorists will find an unwinking barricade across the Bath Road at Slough. In some way at which we can only guess, the dark country gods will wake from their sleep; the forces in the whispering woods and the brooding hills will be abroad, in twentieth-century forms.

Let the townsman recall the name on many of these queer machines—Ruston-Bucyrus. Let him ask the country people out loud, about Bucyrus. *That* will cause a silence, glasses half way to lips.

What is this rustic god, this Bucyrus? What is this sly half-joke about rust, rustic, this suggestion of something like a furnace of Moloch found half-buried, rusting, in the pastoral graveyard of some old civilisation – and yet not dead at all, only *waiting?*

May we not guess that the root of our unease in the country lies in this, that the people know about Bucyrus and will not tell us? True, they see ' What's My Line?' and have the vote. But ever and anon we stumble behind the screen, we get hints of a sinister fellowship. Near a bustling, matter-of-fact city – Coventry – I saw a month or two ago, in a field, a notice-board outlined against the watery Midland sunset. It said:

TRESPASSERS
WILL BE PROSECUTED

By order, Combe, Binley and Warwickshire
Association for the Prosecution of Felons.

It is a fairly safe bet that these felons are not prosecuted in any *ordinary* court. What are those hooded figures with lanterns? What is this slamming of station-wagon doors in a dark lane at dead of night, this converging on a copse in a damp field? What tribunal is this, where obeisances are made to an effigy of the dread Bucyrus, before the shivering felons are dealt with by a society compared with which the Ku-Klux-Klan or the Mau Mau seem like naive, artificial college initiations?

Impossible to tell. Perhaps this is just a ritual developed to express that feeling we have all had, under the summer trees, that to look at the landscape is not enough; we must commune with it, eat it, *be* it. We must make it care about us.

Or perhaps Bucyrus is on the move. Just to be safe, let us watch those machines.

THE GHOST TRAM

Almost every week now some newspaper carries a sad little story of 'The Last Tram Ride,' with a flashlight picture (for it is always 11.3 on Saturday night) of merry youths in paper top hats, carrying rattles. We are sad in a vague way, because there has always been a vague, ghost-like sadness about trams.

Even in their heyday they always had this curiously insubstantial, *potential* quality, as though they were ghostly ideas waiting for realisation. Their lines issued from quiet, mysterious depôts and covered the town like the nervous system for some sixth sense not quite apprehended. They never quite attained the private, solid identity of railways.

One felt there should have been tram *stations*, with flower-beds and waiting-rooms, and attendants in recognisable liveries. But they never became real, they never acquired a folk-lore as trains did. The only evidence of tram-consciousness in ordinary speech that one can recall is the tramlines on a tennis court.

It is true that ' Modern Tramways,' a magazine with over 55,000 readers who care for trams, can recommend ' on a wet day, when inclement weather hinders more active tramway research . . . ' a visit to the Science Museum, which contains ' fine examples of early West Ham cars.' It is true that this magazine can print advertisements like this:

What do you know of Conductors' Brothers-in-law, Return Platform Tickets, the Fair Fare System, Repeat Transfers? Fare collection is a large and fascinating subject with many unexpected facets of the utmost interest to every tram enthusiast. Read all about this intriguing subject in ' The Theory of Fare Collecting,' by W. H. Bett. Now ready for delivery. 8s. 6d. post free.

But we are not convinced. We feel that this appeal is only to specialists, whereas folk-lore appeals to everybody. We cannot imagine a successful play called ' The Ghost Tram.'

And yet, and yet. Now that the people with paper top hats have been seen even at Victoria, and a whole nexus of South London Tramways has disappeared, one of the few remaining routes is the one that connects north and south London by way of the unique tunnel. Here trams disappear at an acute angle into the bowels of the earth at the end of Kingsway, and reappear on the Embankment, under Waterloo Bridge. Now, the time cannot be far off when the future of this tunnel, which is perhaps the nearest trams ever got to having a private life, must be discussed. And I would like to enter a plea that it simply be disused; not sealed off, not opened to petrol traffic; just disused. If this is done I am quite sure there *will* be a Ghost Tram.

The whole situation is most appropriate. The tunnel debouches at a point where ships are sadly moored, ships that will never sail again, ships that listen to mournful sirens on the foggy air, a melancholy doomed call to action that can never be. Across the river is the Festival of Britain, surrounded by gloomy warehouses where once all was light and laughter. One thinks of what might have happened if trams had succeeded; one imagines dim water-trams plying on the Thames; river trams – nay, marine trams.

On the one side of the tunnel are Shell Mex House and the Savoy – the hard, practical sphere of business and buses, success and reality, the gay laughter of elegant diners in the heedless world that has turned away from trams. On the other side is King's College, where intellectuals, scientists and managers, plan the non-tram world of the future.

No, let us have no statues of great tram designers for memorial, no West Ham cars in museums. Let us have this lonely quiet in the heart of London, to be passed, like a haunted churchyard, with fitting trepidation. Let us restrain showmen who might wish to turn it into a vulgar, fairground Ghost Tram, with skeletons, and hanging bits of fur brushing and faces of giggling passengers, and mechanical howls. Let us acknowledge the mystery of the vehicle that never quite got there.

Let us never enter this tunnel. Let us listen with awe and respect at its gloomy entrance, for the elfin clang and silvery rattle that are never quite heard, and look for the far-off flashes of moony electricity that we shall never quite see. Thus shall we best salute an urban spirit that was never quite alive, and will never quite die.

L

THE SPONGE

Although there is not much likelihood of England's ever becoming a Hindu country, there is at least one element of that vast, baffling religion which mirrors a basic truth obvious in the life of modern London and other big cities – the instinct that shop-keepers, the *Vaishya* caste, are in some way subtly different from other people. The size of shop does not matter.

When big metropolitan shops are closed there is a kind of aura of sub-life about them, a suggestion of a heart ticking over. Strictly speaking, the *Vaishya* caste includes bankers and other traders as well as shop-keepers, but the parallel does not extend this far in London. When one goes down to the City on a Sunday it is completely dead. The tide has gone out from the grey cliffs of buildings; one is alone, with bits of old newspaper, on this Sunday beach. One knows that all these banking and insurance people are mowing their lawns and watching the television in Croydon. They have left nothing behind.

But with the shops in the West End it is different. A city is a dream, and there is something strictly surreal about these pianos and percolators and books on the Royal Family and handbags all gathered together so inexplicably, so remote from their real creators and craftsmen. A shop is an insulated dream world, which one can apprehend not by concentration but by diffusion, just as one looks all round, rather than at, a distant star. The moment one concentrates in a shop, this mysterious life vanishes, as witches vanish at cock-crow. But relax, and it comes back.

See, is there not a shadowy, potential community living here, as in a vast house? Four thousand souls, preparing shadowy meals in the basement, among the washing-machines and ironing-boards and crockery; leaving evidence of embryo personalities among the individual bric-a-brac on the ground floor, where a thousand watches tick and stockings are hanging; forever about to get something out of the still, mothballed wardrobes on the quiet first floor, where racks of dresses await the flesh; sleeping calmly on the thousand beds, listening to unheard music from the silent pianos on the third floor, the drawing-room floor with soft piles of carpets . . .

That is in big shops. One might think that smaller shops – shops festooned with small articles on hanging cards, shops of small chemists who disappear for long, silent periods into the dispensary, shops whose owners emerge blinking from small dark parlours when the small bell tinkles – would be more ordinary, more like us. But it is not so. Shop-keepers, *all* of them, are different from us.

What, for instance, are the motives of the small chemist in whose window, in a very humdrum part of London, I saw an enormous sponge, marked £7? Why did he order this thing? And who does he think is going to buy it?

Seven *pounds*. Even the foreign visitors that one always reads about but never sees, walking along Bond Street with their rough prairie ways and their bags of gold dust, would think twice about paying £7 for a sponge.

Is this chemist a romantic, enchanted by the very notion of sponges waving dreamily about to the silent music of the sea floor in some clear Mediterranean pool, marking it at this preposterous £7 because he can't bear the thought of anyone taking it away? Or does he, perhaps, play with more macabre fancies? Does he dream fearfully of the day when the door of his shop is literally darkened, and a giant's head looks in, saying ' I'd like to see some sponges ' in a voice of thunder?

This vast sponge fills half the window as it is: What happens when a man puts it in his bath and it begins to expand, pushing him first up the sloping non-tap end, then bulging out over the bath, filling the bathroom, flattening him against the wall with a vile, lichenous pressure . . .

No, no, the truth is not this way. This sponge is, in fact, a magic, symbolic object. The jars of red and green water show this man's initiation in the more obvious, clear-cut mysteries of chemistry; but the sponge is the symbol of something far more diffuse and vague – of his *Vaishya* membership. He, too, is a shopman, as well as a chemist. He belongs to this marvellous commercial nexus; he is one of these magical middlemen who bring us the fruits of the earth in neat parcels with looped string.

To belong to this caste is to have a mysterious communion with all who convert the brute, material world to our use – a communion in which the smallest shopkeeper is as important as the greatest food scientist or technologist. For I have seen, at the corner of my own street, in a little shop crammed with fly-papers and tin toys and bottles of vinegar and obscure papers and sweets and pinafores, a list of Articles which May Not Be Sold on Sundays; and it includes *aeroplane parts*. We feel that on a Monday, or a Tuesday, it is just possible we might walk in and find a gleaming jet engine lying next to the liquorice all-sorts; just as somebody might walk in and buy that £7 sponge. For the *Vaishya* caste are ready, waiting, inscrutable, behind the counter . . .

CORONATION
WITHOUT QUEUEING

Like all normal people, I look forward to the Coronation;
to that curious, intense silence that comes over London
when the ancient words are uttered in the Abbey; to the
moment when Britain holds its breath before the trumpets
and shouting; the actual Now when the page is turned. It
will not matter then that I am in some back street behind
Charing Cross, wedged between a lamp-post and a
giantess with a giant child on her shoulders.

What does matter is the anxious feeling I have now that
every day splendid chances of actually seeing the procession are passing me by, if only I knew what to do.
Whenever I pick up ' The Times ' there are advertisements
by forceful, enterprising people, snapping up wonderful

first-floor premises; there are accounts of arrangements for sea-scouts from remote countries, for jam champions from the Women's Institutes, for the Akhond of Swat, for schoolchildren, and doubtless for trade unionists and officials of the Ministry of Fuel and Power. Everywhere there is this vast, purposeful scheming, for a huge picnic to which I have not been asked.

No, no, this is absurd. There must be thousands more who feel as I do. For their benefit I offer the results of my search for ways of seeing the Coronation without camping and without belonging to something like the Worshipful Company of Loriners or Vintners. All you need for any of these methods is courage.

STATUE METHOD

The route is dotted with statues. Take the quadriga at the top of Constitution Hill, for instance. Nobody would notice if two or three more people were seated on that rearing horse, like Uncle Tom Cobley's friends, or standing beside it in allegorical attitudes.

Or make your own statue, of canvas with a steel framework, to conceal a party of friends. It would have to be rather a big statue. If this sounds impossible, remember the man who, in the twenties, dug a hole in Piccadilly Circus and invited his friends in there to dine with him.

ELEPHANT METHOD

You could ride up on an elephant quite late on the actual morning and people would make way for you. Hyde Park is the best place for this. I have studied the by-laws, and it says you cannot sing, ring any bell, sound any rattle, or drive a hearse; but it doesn't say anything about elephants. If you have a circus elephant, be careful, as it may want to join the procession.

TUNNEL METHOD

Have lunch every day with your wife until 1st June at a restaurant in Haymarket. If by January you do not know them so well that they *offer* you a place, start tunnelling under the table, passing earth, etc., up to your wife, who should carry a knitting bag for the purpose. Your tunnel should come just inside the road in Haymarket. Look out for high-tension cables, gas mains, etc.

BBC METHOD

You will want a hand microphone and about thirty yards of cable. Push through the crowds to the front, saying, ' What's your name, madam? Have you been here long? Would you like to tell listeners what it's like, here in this vast crowd?' If a policeman asks to see your pass, whisper fiercely, ' We're on the air. My pass is in my jacket in the control van, back there.' (There is sure to be a real control van somewhere near, behind a thirty-deep crowd.)

FOREIGN DELEGATION METHOD

You probably couldn't actually get into the Abbey by this method. But you could get a good seat on the route. You should all be in morning dress, with obscure medals and decorations, and all but one should be made up swarthy. The remaining one should say to a police inspector, ' But this is terrible. I am looking after this delegation and there has been a mistake in the seating plans.' (Then, to your companions, ' *Ugaluga m'humbi balum, M'phm.*') ' Heaven knows what H.E. will say if we lose the trade agreement. Do you think you could just squeeze them on to this stand? (*Ulunda, cha, m'hm m'hm.*)'

BALLOON METHOD

Rather expensive. You will want four balloons, one on

each compass point about four miles away from the route, and a fast car, since you will have to go at the last moment to the one best served by the wind. Beware of landing on bands. If forced down, look perplexed, say ' Isn't this Essex?'

PERISCOPE METHOD

Or just buy a periscope.

HARLEY STREET

I have always thought that if I were a British Council Official showing some Eastern potentate, like the Akhond of Swat or the Zigzag of Gong, round London, I should make him feel at home straight away by pointing out the capital's curious habit of grouping trades together in streets, as they do in Eastern bazaars.

' This is Fleet Street, the Street of Scribes,' I should say, ' and here is Savile Row, the Street of Tailors.' Then there would be Lombard Street, the Street of Money Changers; Hatton Garden, the Street of Diamonds; Chancery Lane, the Street of Lawyers; Warren Street, the Street of Automobile Dealers. And, of course, there would be Harley Street, the Street of Doctors.

Of course, the Zigzag would be disappointed if he

expected to find a roaring, colourful thoroughfare, with doctors sitting cross-legged in open booths and shouting to passers-by ' Sir! I got lovely appendix knife. I cut you up, very cheap, very good.' For Harley Street is nothing if not dignified and quiet. I used to live in a mews at the back of Harley Street, and I was almost the only person in the whole square mile who didn't have a Rolls-Royce.

I bet there's a bigger concentration of Rolls-Royces in Harley Street than anywhere else in the world. There are old, high Rolls-Royces, with solemn, deep horns like the *Queen Mary's* siren. There are shiny, new Rolls-Royces, some painted over with that extraordinary pattern to look like wickerwork. And for the younger, more dashing specialists, there are the nearest that Rolls-Royces ever came to sporting models – those old tourers. As a matter of fact, I'm not at all sure they're all real Rolls-Royces, with engines. I suspect that some of them are just plywood models, with nothing at all inside. They just stand all day for show, and are towed away by horses late at night.

It's a wonder to me how all these Rolls-Royces remain in such good condition, because the Harley Street area is one of the two most dangerous for driving in London. The other is Soho. Both these districts were laid out in the precise, mathematical manner of the Georgians, and both are therefore full of busy right-angle crossings with the views blocked by tall corner buildings.

If you stand around long enough in Soho you are bound to see, from a good vantage point, a taxi and a car converging. You say to yourself ' That taxi's going to hit that car,' and it *does*. It's a wonderful, godlike feeling; but it's even better around Harley Street, because the chances are it'll be two Rolls-Royces.

But more fascinating even than Rolls-Royce crashes, to

the casual bystander in this area, are the shops. I first
noticed them long before I lived anywhere near. I noticed
them when I started going to the Wigmore Hall. This,
naturally enough, is in Wigmore Street, which forms one
boundary of the Doctors' District. All concerts at the
Wigmore Hall end at five minutes past nine, a horribly
empty hour when it's too early to go home and too late to
start anything else.

It is always raining when you come out into Wigmore
Street, that is not quite in the West End; and you drift
about aimlessly, wondering what to do next, when you find
yourself looking at these terrible shops they have for
doctors. Apart from fairly harmless things, like doctors'
bags and those cold horsehair couches they all have, these
shops sell awful things like bent nut-crackers, all chromium-plated and gleaming.

There are chromium-plated saws, and frightful tweezers
and spikes and needles, and things like toast-racks with
knurled screws, for holding the body open while they get
on with whatever they're doing. There are dreadful
extending tubes, like the legs of camera tripods only with
knives and lights at the end. There are even chromium-
plated hammers. There are complicated machines for
giving anaesthetics, complete with chromium-plated
spanners; and lewd, bulging things made of red rubber.

Some shops crowd their windows with these horrors.
Others just have a table-cloth laid out with one chromium-
plated mincer lying tastefully on it, like the one hat in a
Bond Street milliner's. And there is one shop where they
have all these things only *four times as big*, for veterinary
surgeons.

It was only when I saw all this stuff, some of which is made
on the premises, that I began to realise that this is a district

of craftsmen, too, to realise that there are people who spend their whole lives making these de-luxe tools. The other day I saw a letter in a magazine called *Packaging*, a very tasteful publication, which is usually full of bright suggestions for cornflake packets or toothpaste caps so ingenious that the public will be practically forced to buy whatever brand adopts them. This letter was headed:

CONTAINERS FOR HUMAN ORGANS

Sir,

We are suppliers of every type of equipment for hospitals and other public bodies and institutions, and are at present seeking alternatives to the 5 in. by $7\frac{1}{2}$ in. diameter waxed containers, which we cannot now obtain.

These are required to hold human organs for short periods, must of course be completely watertight and have a tight-fitting lid, and be of approximately the capacity indicated by the measurements quoted above. Any suggestions you can make will be greatly appreciated by ourselves and by hospital authorities throughout the country.

Why five inches by seven-and-a-half inches? You couldn't get a human *leg* in a container that size. But I bet you could get them all sizes in those shops around Harley Street. I bet you could get them five by seven-and-a-half *feet*. I bet you could get *anything* in those shops.

In the artistes' room at the Wigmore Hall, among the signed photographs of Kreisler and Paderewski, there is a picture of a man in sober Edwardian clothes standing beside what looks like an enormous Meccano model, in the middle of which is what looks like a violin. In fact it *is* a violin, and this is a machine for playing it, a violin version of the pianola.

Well, I wouldn't mind betting that this contraption started life in some workshop at the back of Harley Street, as a help to some devilish operation. And then after a few people had died the man changed it into a violin-playing machine – cat guts instead of people's. They're clever, those people in Harley Street.